WOGGLE AND

BUTTER HARSIES

Overleaf: *The old postmill which stood in the grounds of Mill House. Partly hidden by the mill is the weather-boarded granary in which the Young Mariners for many years practised their Christmas carols before making the rounds of the town.*

WOGGLE AND BUTTER HARSIES

Life in an Essex marshland village

GEORGE CLARKE

TERENCE DALTON LIMITED
LAVENHAM, SUFFOLK 1990

Published by
TERENCE DALTON LIMITED
ISBN 0 86138 081 9
© George Clarke, 1990

Text photoset in 10/11pt Baskerville
Printed in Great Britain at
The Lavenham Press Limited, Lavenham, Suffolk

Contents

Preface

The plan on the opposite page shows Burnham as it was about the turn of the century. It was drawn by Paul Malster.

Burnham is seen en fête *in this view of High Street from the entrance to the Maltings Yard. Possibly the occasion was the celebrations of the Coronation of King Edward VII in 1902.*

HAVING found a good deal of interest in the paperback *Burnham-on-Crouch in the 1800s* I realized that much has happened in the first five decades of the twentieth century which also warrants being put on record. The realization, too, that those born in the town with a living memory of those early days are steadily getting fewer and fewer has given some urgency to my attempt to write a follow-up.

Burnham is the town of my birth, and of my father's and grandfather's, and the town in which I have spent eighty years. Practically all my working life was spent in the office of the local newspaper, the *Burnham-on-Crouch and Dengie Hundred Advertiser*, which was last published in 1971 (I started as "Printer's Devil" in

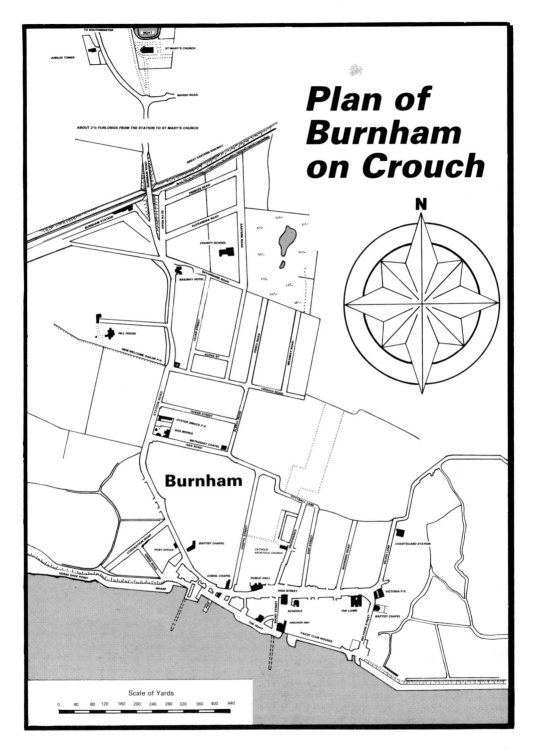

Plan of
Burnham
on Crouch

N

Burnham

TO SOUTHMINSTER

JUBILEE TOWER

ST MARY'S CHURCH

MARSH ROAD

ABOUT 2½ FURLONGS FROM THE STATION TO ST MARY'S CHURCH

GREAT EASTERN RAILWAY

BURNHAM STATION

PRINCES ROAD

ALEXANDRA ROAD

COUNTY SCHOOL

DEVONSHIRE ROAD

RAILWAY HOTEL

HILL HOUSE

NEW WELCOME SAILOR P.H.

ALPHA ST

CROUCH ROAD

QUEEN STREET

OYSTER SMACK P.H.

GAS WORKS

METHODIST CHAPEL

GAS ROAD

STATION ROAD

BAPTIST CHAPEL

CATHOLIC APOSTOLIC CHURCH

POST OFFICE

CONG CHAPEL

PUBLIC HALL

HIGH STREET

SCHOOLS

THE LAWN

COASTGUARD STATION

VICTORIA P.H.

BAPTIST CHAPEL

HORSE SHOE POINT

WHARF

THE QUAY

ANCHOR INN

YACHT CLUB HOUSES

CORONATION ROAD

Scale of Yards

0   40   80   120   160   200   240   280   320   360   400   440

Left: *Cupola House in High Street, which became the Burnham Working Men's Institute. It contained a reading room, public baths and a billiards room; the latter became the council chamber when the property was acquired by the town council.*
Below: *Pannell's Mill in Mill Road, demolished in the early years of this century. At one time the cottage in the background was occupied by the Gardner family.*

The sea wall looking east towards the wharf, with Cranfield's sail loft prominent on the left. In the middle distance is the Royal Corinthian Yacht Club, destroyed by fire in 1914.

1924 and spent several years in the editor's chair before retiring); this ensured that I have been constantly in touch with happenings and developments in the town. Such a grounding must surely stand me in good stead in the task which I have set myself.

I consider it both a privilege and a pleasure to write of Burnham as it was before the "planners" and developers took a hand, but it is a task I approach with some trepidation as I do not find it easy to dismiss from my mind the fear that although I have deliberately spread my net wide there may yet be facets of life in the town during the period under review which will elude me. There is certainly much of interest in the town's history which should go on record now, while the "oldsters", from whom much of the information must come, are still with us.

My aim is not a literary masterpiece and I am no historian, so what I am attempting is more in the nature of a simple record of life and events in the days of my childhood and youth.

In the knowledge that memory is dimmed by time I appreciate that my version of various subjects may differ from that of my contemporaries. I do not claim that versions are necessarily the correct ones; they are simply the facts as I remember them.

I am grateful to those who have so readily provided any necessary data and I take this opportunity to place on record my appreciation and thanks for the kindly advice, encouragement and help given me by Mr Hervey Benham, of Essex County Newspapers, and to my granddaughter Sharon for so painstakingly typing the manuscript.

My hope is that the book will prove both interesting and readable, and that some will find passages to stir long-forgotten memories of those bygone halcyon days.

The Old Order 1 Changeth

THERE can be few more momentous years in history than the first seven decades of the twentieth century—seventy years which saw two world wars, the advent of atomic power, the introduction of that great world shrinker, air travel, and the first landing on the moon. But something that has probably had more personal effect on most of us is the population explosion, which has necessitated the taking over of large tracts of land for the erection of new towns, and increasing development in existing towns and villages, in order to cope with the insatiable demand for more and more homes.

The pressure of development has greatly affected Burnham-on-Crouch, although the older part of the town, nearer the river, is little changed from how it looked at the turn of the century.

In the High Street, which is full of character and charm, the only concessions which have been allowed to the demands of the developers and "progress" are the regrettable demolition of The Lawns and the controversial High Street Improvement Scheme in 1963, which in effect amounted to little more than the repainting of several properties, the removal of the louvres in the top of the Clock Tower, the formation of flower beds and the planting of half a dozen trees. This was not the first time the town's broad High Street had boasted trees. Until well into the 'forties a row of limes stretched down the middle of the street from Warners Hall almost to the Constitutional Club. It was in the shade of these trees that the children of the town were given a tea to celebrate the end of the 1914–18 war.

The Lawns, which was on the site of the present Belvedere Estate, was a fine old red brick property standing in spacious well kept grounds with immaculate lawns. For a great many years it was the residence of the Auger family, who were people of some standing in the town and owners of oyster layings. The last of the line was Mr Johnny Auger, a great cricketer with the reputation of being the most exasperating "stone-waller" in the district.

Outside the older part of the town, Burnham has greatly changed. Until fifty or sixty years ago the only buildings on the western side of Station Road between Station Approach and Mill

Opposite page:
Burnham railway station in its very early days before the building of the Mildmay Ironworks on the open ground to the left.

House were a shop and cottage on Foundry Lane corner, Egypt Cottage (occupied in those days by the Gadsdon family and now part of Winstree Estate), and Hill House, the residence in turn of the Rogers and Ridsdale families, later converted by Mr H. Bilborough into the Hill House Residential Hotel and finally demolished, its site becoming part of the Winstree Estate. The site now occupied by the United Reformed Church and the other buildings between the public footpath to Creeksea and Winstree Road was part of the extensive and attractive grounds of Hill House. An unbroken row of mature trees, mainly elms, stretched from Foundry Lane to the present library site, and for many years contained a rookery.

The buildings from the top of the hill to the library, the Hillside Road properties east of Park Road and Burnham Hillside Bowls Club rinks, are all on what was then known as Hill Field, which was virtually a public playing field, on which a herd of cows from Hill

Hill House was at one time the residence of the Rogers and Ridsdale families and then became an hotel. Its extensive grounds are now covered by the Winstree Estate.

Farm (then farmed by Percy Pipe) occasionally grazed. It was on Hill Field that Mildmay Ironworks Football Club played their home matches before they moved to Mildmay Sports Ground. Beside the road at the top end of the field was a double row of trees with a well-trodden space between. This was known, to youngsters at least, as the "Forest" and it was here we played such games as kicky-man-policeman and relievo. A more open space was required for two other favourite games, woggle and billymot. During the 1914–18 war Hill Field was taken over by an artillery battery stationed in the town. It was here that the horses and mules were turned out and marquees and a cookhouse erected, the soldiers themselves being billeted in the town.

Separated from Hill Field by a wide well-filled ditch was Mill Field, on which Warwick Court, Burnham Sports Club's pavilion, the Scouts' hut and Millfields now stand. It was here that Burnham Ramblers Football Club played their home matches until they moved to Silver Road in 1926.

Much used by youngsters as a play area was a field at the rear of Prospect Place where a tennis club later had its courts. The site was eventually sold to become Remembrance Avenue. The gravel pits in Arcadia Road (now Dunlin Haven Estate) were also used by youngsters as common land, as was Cats Wood (which adjoined the railway and is now within the grounds of St Mary's Primary School in Marsh Road) and Martin's Meadow (a field between the Orchard Road end of Ship Road and Riverside Road). There was also a sizable open space, including a sandpit at the end of Princes Road, adjoining the railway line, much used as a play area by the "up streeters", whose stamping ground also included a rough tract of land covered with furze bushes on the east side of Eastern Road, stretching from the Iron Bridge to opposite the Alexandra Road junction. This area was known as "Stammers", no doubt on account of the fact that an old man by that name had his pig sties there. The north end of this area was later taken over as a factory site by the Burnham Preserving Company, known locally as the jam factory. During the Second World War the premises (which later became the council depot) were used as ARP headquarters and fire station. Council bungalows now occupy this site.

Orchard Road used to end at the Ship Road junction, but there was a footpath which crossed Martin's Meadow and passed a pair of black weatherboarded cottages known as The Barracks and came out into Silver Road. Martin's Meadow, in which there was a pond (usually cluttered up with rubbish), was regularly hired by fun fair and circus proprietors. Other pitches were at the gravel pits on the site now occupied by the Carnival Hall, Brickwall Field (now Brickwall Close) and Mill Field, and on regatta days a fair would squeeze into the Maltings Yard. Some of the roundabouts in those days were motivated by a hapless horse which was harnessed up to the inner side of the wooden horses and driven round and round. Names of fair proprietors springing readily to mind are Bibby, Gumble and Hedges, and Fossetts was probably the best known travelling circus to visit the town.

In my younger days Albert Road and Chapel Road skirted fields, there being no buildings on their east side apart from the dwellings between the High Street and the Witney Road junction. Dorset Road, Alamein Road, Arnhem Road and Dunkirk Road were to come much later. It was in one of these Chapel Road dwellings that Burnham's first telephone exchange was sited.

The site now occupied by White Wings, the residence of Mrs Warwick Smith, was then the boatyard of the redoubtable Harvey Brothers—John, Ike, Jim and Bill—four dour characters who owned the pleasure boats *Favourite* and *Water Lily* in which day trippers, of which there were many in those days, were taken for trips and in which they made the weekly journey to Foulness to take groceries, meat, and clothing to the islanders.

The site of Dilliway Court at the junction of Station Road and Western Road originally housed the town's gasworks. It was here that as youngsters we watched with awe as the workmen, stripped to the waist and with rivulets of sweat running down their dust-grimed faces, raked out the white-hot coals from the retorts and drenched them with buckets of water, sending up clouds of sulphurous fumes which soon had those who ventured too close gasping for air. It was here, too, that mothers sent to play any of their brood suffering from whooping cough, the belief being that these pungent fumes had a remedial effect on this now-far-less-common scourge. The gasworks site, from which coke could be purchased for about tenpence per bushel, became an animated scene on Saturday mornings when youngsters turned up to collect this then-widely-used commodity in a bizarre assortment of old perambulators, home-made box carts, and wheelbarrows. Dominating the site was a large gasometer which reared its unsightly bulk only a few feet from both Station Road and Western Road.

Maple Leaf Estate was formerly an orchard. When I was a youngster the only house in Maldon Road between the Church Road junction and Ostend were Cherry Gardens, Pinners and the cottage adjoining it. On the opposite side of the road on the site now occupied by Maldon Road Garage was a large black weatherboarded barn owned by an estate agent by the name of Suter, who owned a fair bit of property in that area and had a tiny office in Station Approach. Adjoining the two old cottages which stand back from the road on the left hand side before reaching the George and Dragon was a corrugated iron building used as an isolation hospital.

Public Services   2

I WONDER how many of us stop to consider, when the strident notes of a fire engine are heard, how fighting a fire was done in the early part of the century. These were the days before firemen were summoned by the wail of a siren, when personal alerters now carried by every fireman were undreamt of: the pre-telephone days.

When a fire occurred at night outside the town—as most fires did—the alarm was raised by someone cycling to Burnham to notify the police, who in turn notified the captain of the fire brigade, who would then don his uniform and make a round of the town calling out the other members of the brigade. In the meantime someone would be despatched to contact a driver, whose task it was to secure a pair of horses—a pair were usually kept "on call" for this purpose—and get them harnessed to the manual fire engine, garaged at the lower end of the town in a building which also housed the morgue, on the site now occupied by public lavatories.

These preliminaries were especially time-consuming at night, when those involved were abed and the horses had been turned out to graze. In the case of a marsh farm fire the journey was in itself quite a hazardous task for the person sent to raise the alarm, for he had probably only an oil lamp to light his way, and gates across the road at frequent intervals had to be opened and closed to prevent cattle and horses straying.

For the firemen, getting to the scene of the blaze was often a hair-raising dash; on one occasion one of the firemen was so apprehensive about the journey ahead that rather than face the hazards he is alleged to have taken a chance and jumped off as the horses eased slightly breasting Old Farm Hill on the way to a marsh farm fire. On arrival the first task was to locate an adequate supply of water, because no water was carried on the old manual engine and it had to be manoeuvred close enough to the pond or ditch for the limited length of suction hose to be used. The long pump handles—one on each side—which when opened out stretched the entire length of the appliance and beyond, were then manned and the task of pumping began, with anything up to eight pumpers on each side.

This was a task in which the firemen were always glad of help from the public. Those who did lend a hand had their names recorded by one of the firemen and for their services eventually received payment (I think it was half a crown), which had to be collected from the Council Offices. I remember qualifying for two such payments: one was for pumping at a disastrous Saturday night fire that destroyed Newman's grocery and hardware store in High Street, when members of the public also helped remove some of the stock, and the other for pumping at a stack fire at Cherry Gardens, then farmed by Mr Horrobin.

Great changes in street lighting have been made in the town. It was in 1898 that a meeting of ratepayers was held at the National School to levy a rate for lighting the parish for one year by gas. The envisaged scheme was for the lighting of the whole of the town from the railway station to Belvedere Road with fifty-two lamps. At this time there was a total of 634 houses in the parish. The meeting decided that the sum of £165 be granted to the lighting inspectors to meet the lighting expenses for one year. The rateable value of the town was then £3,750 and the lighting rate one shilling in the pound. The average distance between the lamps would be rather under one hundred yards, which was less than at either Chelmsford or Maldon.

The lamps were lit individually each night by men walking round with a ladder and a box of matches—no easy task on a windy

Burnham's manual fire engine in action at a fire in High Street in the early years of the century. The Shand Mason appliance required at least eight men aside to work the pump.

One of the old gas lamps in High Street rising out of the floodwater; an abnormally high tide in November, 1897, inundated much of the lower part of the town.

night—and the same men again made the rounds later at night to turn each lamp out. The two lamplighters I can first remember were Josiah Willett and "Tinny" Cole. Electricity did not come to Burnham until 1926.

In these days, when every house in the town is on the main sewer, it is difficult to believe that only a few decades ago a great many cottages still had only pail closets. These were primitive little wooden constructions like sentry boxes, usually at the bottom of long gardens—not particularly inviting to jump out of bed and run to on a dark frosty night! The last of these pail closets to go were those in low-lying areas including Prospect Place and Coronation Road.

The "night cart", as it was familiarly known—a large horse-drawn tank slung between two large wheels—did its rounds in the early morning, thankfully before many people were astir. In the winter months on the way to start work at the old *Advertiser* office at seven o'clock in the morning I often had the misfortune to pass the night cart as it slopped its way along Prospect Place, and the smell was off-putting to say the least. But Harry Chitticks, a bearded old character and a great tobacco chewer, seemed to make light of his job. Later in the day he would be seen round the town with the same horse but a different cart—this time the dust cart, emptying dustbins. This was an operation which caused clouds of dust to fly —small wonder it was called the dustcart. And this was in the days when uncovered foodstuffs, particularly meat and greengrocery, were on display outside the shops.

This scavenging was carried out not by the council but by a private contractor, local farmer Mr Wilfred Newman, whose charge for emptying the pail closets and the dustbins was £135 a year, or £2 12s a week. He had two tips for dustbin rubbish: one an old sandpit in Maldon Road at the rear of "Pantiles" and the other on what is now Pippins Estate off Eastern Road.

Around the turn of the century, when Burnham's population was in the region of 3,000, the town had a better postal delivery service than that in operation half a century and more later, when the population was nearer 5,000. In the early nineteen-hundreds the postmaster was Mr H. T. Bull and the Post Office was in High Street. In the winter months there were three town deliveries daily, starting at 7.10 am, 11 am and 4 pm, the postmen each carrying a lamp for the evening round. Dispatches were at 11.10 am, 2.05 pm (Saturdays 1.45 pm), 5.50 pm and 7.10 pm, and there was also a Sunday collection. The telegraph office was open from 8 am until 8 pm (Sundays 8 am until 10 am).

A horse-drawn mail van arrived from Maldon each weekday morning but all the rest of the town's mail arrived and was dispatched by rail. The local mail was franked and sorted at the Burnham office and transported to and from the railway station by postmen using a hand truck. Postmen were also responsible for collecting the mail from the various pillar boxes in their district.

Among the postmen were William Robinson and Elijah Clarke, who were responsible for the town deliveries for many years before the increase in the volume of mail necessitated an extra roundsman and Harold Rouse joined the staff. When Elijah Clarke first started the job he was allocated the marsh round, which he did on foot on alternate days, no cycle being provided by the authorities. This round was later taken over by Mr Raven, who wisely used his own cycle, which at least must have made the long trip to Holliwell Farm and Coney Hall less irksome.

In those days Wallasea Island was included in the Burnham postal district, and delivering mail round this sparsely populated island of dykes and grassland, used almost entirely for grazing sheep and cattle, was the unenviable task of Mr Walter Hopgood, who was by no means a young man. Each morning he was rowed across the river by local waterman Mr Frank Bailey and put ashore at Grapnells Point, to be picked up and returned to the town steps when his round, which entailed much walking by seawall, farm tracks and field paths, was completed.

For many years deliveries in the Ostend, Green Lane–Mangapps–Stoneyhills district were made by Stanley Clarke, the son of Elijah Clarke.

Throughout the years covered by this book Burnham was kept well posted with what was going on in the district by the four-page weekly *Burnham-on-Crouch and Dengie Hundred Advertiser*, affectionately dubbed the "Burnham Rag", or the "Duster". In the Bradwell area I frequently heard it referred to as the "Burnham Buster". The first edition appeared in 1904, the founder and first editor being Ebenezer Dilliway, a native of Burnham, who first got ink into his blood when employed by one of the county newspapers.

His premises, which I understand were formerly used as a

The staff of Burnham Post Office in Station Road in 1930. At left are postmen Harold Rouse and William Robinson; Mrs Ryan, the postmistress, stands in the middle, and next to her is Miss Rita Tunbridge (now the author's wife), with Miss Ellen Stebbings leaning against the shop window.

laundry, were in Providence behind a row of wooden cottages opposite the Queen's Head, of which at that time the licensee was Mrs Sarah Read. The printing machine was a hand-operated Ingle flatbed, which also did service for poster printing. On publication days a man was employed solely to turn the handle; the machine could almost be likened to a king-size clothes wringer or mangle. The paper was hand folded, and the type for both news and advertisements was hand set. The original price of one halfpenny remained until around 1918, when the "Halfpenny Rag" became the "Penny Duster".

A remarkable man, Mr Dilliway was also secretary of Burnham Gas Company and clerk to Burnham Urban District Council. It was thus almost to be expected that Burnham council meetings, at which it was not uncommon for discussion to become somewhat heated, should be reported almost verbatim, as well as proceedings at Southminster Petty Sessions. Both on occasions provided some highly amusing reading.

Much of the district news was gathered by "Old Eb", as he was affectionately known, on a weekly cycle tour of the Dengie Hundred. He once confided in me that he gathered most of the items from vicars and ministers, who he claimed "did not miss much of what went on in their parish". Letters to the editor, often

Station Road about 1908, with the long-vanished chestnut trees at the entrance to Coronation Road and the old pump which stood by the roadside in front of St Mary's Hall. Here new premises for the Burnham-on-Crouch and Dengie Hundred Advertiser *were built in the twenties.*

couched in the most provocative terms well laced with colourful adjectives, together with Old Eb's weekly column, "A look round by a Native" (a straight-from-the-shoulder expression of his views on local matters), were always a source of interest. But first to be read was the "hatch, match and despatch" column, which because of the community being so closely knit became almost a personal column.

In the early nineteen-twenties new offices were built in Station Road adjoining St Mary's Hall. Here new machinery was installed and the *Advertiser* was printed on a power-driven Wharfedale flatbed while the Ingle was relegated to poster work only. But the weekly paper was still folded by hand and the type hand set.

About this time Mr Dilliway was joined by his son Leonard, who "covered" the district on a motor cycle and also took over the commercial printing side of the business, which was rapidly expanding and had a workforce of around a dozen. Mr Dilliway junior later left to start his own printing establishment in London.

When in the nineteen-forties Mr Dilliway retired Mr H. A. Savage, local correspondent for the *Essex Weekly News*, became editor of the *Advertiser*, and on his death in 1958 it became my lot to take the editor's chair. This I occupied until 1971, when the *Advertiser* merged with the *Maldon and Burnham Standard* of Essex County Newspapers.

The front page and "masthead" of the Burnham-on-Crouch and Dengie Hundred Advertiser, *of which the author was editor from 1958 to 1971. In earlier days the title had been printed in a much more "modern" typeface.*

11

Industries   3

THROUGHOUT the seventeenth century and well into the eighteenth century the oyster industry was Burnham's biggest employer of labour, with more than 300 workers. For reasons including severe winters, disease and limpets, the local industry has since declined dramatically.

In the early days, when the industry was booming, ownership of the oyster fisheries was of the utmost importance and the source of much controversy. In 1789 the following cautionary warning to oyster dredgers was issued by Lady Mildmay:

> A caution to oyster dredgers.—Whereas Dame Ann Mildmay, the Widow and relict of Sir William Mildmay, Baronet, is the lawful owner of a separate fishery in the waters and streams called Burnham River, otherwise Wallfleet, extending from the west end of a certain place in the said river called or known by the name of Clay Clods, down to another place in the said river called or known by the name of Ray Sand in the main in the County of Essex; and her Ladyship having received undoubted information that many disorderly persons have given out and threatened that they will enter into the said separate Fishery and dredge for oysters, and also enter upon the Oyster Beds in or near the said Fishery and take away the oysters there found, being the sole property of the tenants or lessees, Notice is hereby given, that her Ladyship, on behalf of herself, and of her tenants or lessees is determined to prosecute with the utmost severity of the law, all persons whatsoever who shall enter the said separate fishery, or any of the waters or streams thereto belonging, and dredge for, or take and carry away any of the Oysters or Brood of Oysters, there found, or that shall enter upon the Oyster-beds, in or near the said fishery, and take, spoil or destroy the said Oyster-beds, or any of the Oysters or Brood of Oysters therein.

These layings were later let to Hawkins and Company, of Burnham, and in 1806 the firm had trouble from oyster poachers from Brightlingsea and as a result issued the following caution:

> Caution to Oyster Dredgers.—Whereas information having been received by Messrs. Hawkins and Co., of Burnham, Oyster Dredgers, who occupy under Sir Henry Mildmay, Bart., and Dame Jane, his wife, the Fishery in the river called Burnham River, otherwise Wall Fleet, extending from the west end of a certain place there called Clay Clods, to a place called Ray Sand Head, and on the Raysand in the Main Sea,

that an unlawful combination has been entered into by several Oyster Dredgers in and near Brightlingsea, for the purpose of coming into the said Fishery in a large Body, and by Force, dredging for Oysters therein, and carrying away the same, the property of the said Hawkins and Co.

Notice is hereby given, that the said Fishery is the undoubted Private Property of the said Sir H. Mildmay, and Dame Jane, his wife; and that the same hath been enjoyed by them and their ancestors, without interruption, from the time of King Edward the First, by whom it was first granted; and that all Persons who shall come into the said Fishery, and by Force, dredge therein for oysters, will be guilty of a misdemeanour, and will be punishable by law accordingly. And if any Person or Persons, in a body or individually, shall, without Authority, attempt to dredge in the said Fishery for Oysters, he or they will be prosecuted for the same with the utmost Rigour of the Law.

This warning went unheeded and oyster poaching continued, culminating in a test case being heard at Chelmsford Assizes in March, 1808. It was a most important case for those involved in the oyster fishery, for the judgment would either uphold or disprove the exclusive rights to the oyster fishery of the Burnham River claimed by Sir Henry Mildmay. This, it seemed, was a trial to end all trials; copies of records of three previous trials of the same rights of fishery in the reigns of Charles I and Charles II were mentioned.

By these it appeared that the Earl of Sussex, and after him his Countess of Sussex, and the Lord Fitzwalter, one of the ancestors of the Mildmays, had obtained two verdicts with judgment in confirmation of their right. The court orders showed that the various licences to fish in the Burnham River and also leases had been granted from that early period down to the present time. Many "ancient and respectable" people were then called to prove the long usage of right exclusively exercised by the tenantry of the Mildmay family in the Burnham River from a point called Clay Clods, above Fambridge Ferry, down to the Raysand Beacon, which lies on the main sea.

On behalf of the defendant it was contended that the Burnham River, being an arm of the sea, could not belong to the Manor of Burnham and therefore was free and open for the use of the King's subjects; and as no grant of the Crown had been set forth it was clear that none existed, and therefore no exclusive right could legally be sustained. Counsel concluded by observing that he did not mean to deprive Sir Henry Mildmay of his fair rights in the River Burnham, but contended that the power to exclude the King's subjects from their common rights therein was not vested in Sir Henry Mildmay.

In his summing up Mr Justice Heath said he had no doubt in his mind. He could not remember an ancient right more clearly

Above: This swordfish jawbone, two feet six inches long, commemorates the successful conclusion of a court case in which the rights of owners of the oyster beds in Burnham River were upheld.

14

substantiated both by documents and living witnesses, and he trusted this would prevent any further contests and that the matter had been set to rest for ever. The jury returned a verdict for the owner of the layings for nominal damages and forty shillings costs. To commemorate victory in the case, the successful party had a permanent reminder made in the form of the toothed jaw of a swordfish bearing the words "Burnham Cause, gained March 9th, 1808". At the next Assizes ten men were remanded for trial, six of whom were fishermen, for committing depredations on oyster layings in Burnham River. It seems very strange that not once in these old documents or at any time during the trial was the river called the River Crouch. In the older documents we see it referred to as Burnham River and later as Wallfleet, but never River Crouch.

A former Burnham industry no longer carried on is brickmaking. For many years, until the late nineteen-thirties, there were two brickfields in Green Lane. That on the south side of the road was owned by Mr A. B. Croxon, whose chief employees were members of the Blowers and Partridge families. On the opposite side of the road was the brickfield owned by the Pitcher family, whose main workers were the Farrow family and George Hopkins. The brickmaking process began with the pug being dug and mixed with water until it was of a malleable consistency. The bricks were then hand moulded. The price for this process ranged from 6s 6d to 12s per 1,000, and a good moulder could turn out up to 1,500 per day. The moulded bricks were taken on a specially constructed long

The paddle steamer Jumbo, *which with her sister ship* Alice *was engaged in oyster dredging on the Crouch in the first two decades of this century.*

15

wheelbarrow and stacked in long rows, leaving a space between each brick for drying. When ready they were stacked in a circular dome-shaped kiln, with fire holes around its base. After firing they were left for a couple of days to cool off and were then ready for use. The bricks were red in colour and of a good quality. Multi-reds could be produced by adding manganese to the fires. Production ceased at the outbreak of the 1939–45 war because of the black-out regulations which made it impossible for the kilns to be fired. A paragraph from the early files of the *Burnham Advertiser* states that two Burnham lads were injured when a brick kiln on Brickwall Field collapsed, which indicates that brickmaking was also at one time carried out in the heart of the town.

Nowadays it is difficult to imagine a town without a launderette, but it is not so many years ago that such boons were undreamt of. In former years the nearest Burnham came to this modern convenience was a hand laundry run by Mr and Mrs Spencer. This nice old couple lived in an old cottage which stood on the site now occupied by the Rio Cinema. Their laundry was behind a high brick wall stretching from where the Salvation Army Citadel now stands to almost opposite the Coronation Road junction. The washing was collected and delivered by Mr Spencer, who was almost blind. Wearing his bowler hat and carrying a wicker basket, he was a familiar figure in the town.

From the day it was founded in 1899 by J. W. Booth until it was closed down in 1981, the Burnham firm to employ the most labour

Some of the first employees at Mildmay Ironworks, pictured not long after it opened in 1899. Some of the men in the photograph remained with the firm all their working lives.

Mildmay Ironworks seen from Foundry Lane. The business closed in 1981 and the site is now occupied by a supermarket, offices and new factories.

was Booth and Brookes Ltd (Mildmay Ironworks), whose foundry and offices were in Foundry Lane on the site on which a supermarket and industrial buildings have since been erected. Booth and Brookes' greatest claim to fame is as producers of piano frames, for which they enjoyed a world-wide reputation. On the death of its founder the firm came under the management of his two sons, Sir Paul Booth and C. C. Booth, and it was the latter's two sons, P. C. and J. R. Booth, and W. Earp, Sir Paul's son-in-law, who held the reins when the firm closed down. Although piano frames were originally the firm's main output, a wide variety of castings including gramophone turntables and components for bacon cutting machines were also produced. During the 1914–18 war and the 1939–45 war castings included both shell and hand grenade cases.

Over the years other firms have come and gone, including Burnham Preserving Company, whose works were at the northern end of Eastern Road next to the railway line, and who employed mainly female labour. When the factory was closed down it remained unoccupied for a time before becoming a Burnham council depot. During the war years the premises were used as a fire station and ARP headquarters. At one time, too, there was a potted meat and paste factory in the town with premises on a site since taken over by the Royal Burnham Yacht Club. But this did not flourish for many years and has long since closed down.

Many of the dredgermen from the oyster industry—known

17

locally as "overlanders" because they were ferried across the river, walked to Paglesham at the other side of Wallasea Island, and after the day's work did the journey in reverse—were later employed at the various boatyards. But the labour force in this field has been considerably depleted since the introduction of fibreglass hulls. Sailmaking, too, has been carried out in the town for very many years. In the early days much of the work in the sail lofts was connected with barges, some of which were owned on the Crouch. When these huge barge sails were given a dressing of "tanning" (I believe that is the name it was known by), which was applied by tar brushes, they were spread out in a field, much-used spots for this rather messy task being Martin's Meadow and the corner of the playing field on which Burnham Sailing Clubhouse now stands.

Until well into the present century, before the completion of the Wickford–Southminster branch line, when road transport was still in its infancy and the only power-driven vehicle to visit Burnham was Marriage's steam-driven flour transporter, much more depended on river transport than it does today.

Vessels bringing coal from the north of England coalfields were off-loaded at Prior's Wharf, but it was the humble sailing barge which was the mainstay of the local coastal trade. These stoutly constructed craft, manned by a crew of two—the skipper and his mate, with often a dog aboard—were ideally designed for this type of transport, their shallow draught enabling them to be taken close inshore for either loading or off-loading.

But with the passing years the working barges have gone, in common with the working horses of the farms; both have, it seems, outlived their usefulness. No more, alas, is to be seen the unforgettable sight of these lovely old craft making their way under sail and so deeply laden with a stacked high cargo of baled hay as to leave virtually no visible freeboard, creating the illusion of a stack of baled hay under sail.

The hay was transported to London to provide feed for the many horses then still in use in the metropolis. The barges would seldom return light and often brought in loads of flint or rocks for road making or seawall repairs, fertilizer, coal or cement. In those days it was not uncommon to see up to a dozen barges laden with hay moored in the lower reaches of the Crouch waiting for a favourable wind. When lying windbound, sometimes for days on end, it was not unknown for the bargemen to row ashore to walk the marsh fields in the hope of bagging a hare—then quite plentiful—or some other tasty morsel with which to provide something different for the pot.

Both the loading and off-loading of the cargoes was a demanding manual operation. An insight into just how demanding and back-breaking a task this really was I have learnt from Burnham-

Above: A stackie barge with its cargo of hay built up high above the deck. Because of the deck cargo one member of the crew had to con the ship from atop the stack, shouting instructions down to the other man at the helm.

born Spencer Cole, who was one of a gang of four that undertook this work at Prior's Wharf in the nineteen-twenties. Barges at that time familiar in these waters included *Daisy Maud*, *Mayland*, *Nellie Parker*, *Veronica*, and *Water Lily*, some of which were crewed by local watermen including Dyall Webb, Ernie Cardnell, Len (Pegger) Turner, Harry Turner, and Jimmy Dean. There were also Burnham barge skippers operating in other waters and making the cross-Channel run, and these included Mr Crix and his sons Charlie and Leslie (the latter a schoolday pal of mine who was drowned at sea while still a young man), Mr Paine and Mr Withams.

The gang of four were all natives of the town, who could hardly have claimed to have been overpaid when at the conclusion of their two days of toil in unloading the 120-ton freight of stone brought in by the barge *Mayland* they received £6 14s—to be split four ways!

Roadmaking and -repairing material was the main freight arriving at Burnham by barge, almost entirely for local use. The hundreds of tons of flint purchased by Burnham Council to build up Marsh Road, which hitherto was little more than a deeply-rutted cart track almost impassable except by horse-drawn farm vehicles, arrived by Clement Parker's fleet of barges and was off-loaded at Prior's Wharf.

A cargo which Spencer recalled with distaste was that landed by *Veronica* and *Water Lily*, a combined load of 280 tons of tarmac for use on the notorious stretch of road between Burnham and

The horse ferry at Creeksea on which both horses and cattle crossed the River Crouch. On this occasion the sweep is a passenger.

19

Althorne, now widely known as the "Althorne bends". This sizable task called for five days of unremitting toil, for which their financial reward was £5 per man. The weather being hot at the time, the fumes which emanated from this pungent cargo made the atmosphere in the confines of the holds far from pleasant. How welcome to the team of unloaders must have been the first appearance, as they dug deeper and deeper into the black mass, of the "ceiling", as the bottom of the hold is known to the crew.

All the freight was off-loaded into horse-drawn farm tumbrils, although on one occasion, Spencer recalled, a two-ton motor lorry was also used. The procedure adopted by the gang of unloaders was to have two men in the hold loading the 35–40 lb capacity baskets while the other pair, wearing specially designed home-made hessian garments covering the top of the head and protecting the back, held in place by a tie round the chest, ran the baskets up a short ladder to the deck and along a plank to the wharf and the waiting tumbrils. The gang worked in half-hour shifts, equally sharing the tasks of loading and running.

On the occasions when two barges berthed on the same tide they were moored close alongside each other, and when the barge occupying the wharfside berth (which was the first to be unloaded) happened to be cleared of her cargo when the tide was out, a fifty-foot plank had to be brought into use to unload the vessel occupying the outside berth. Running the whipping fifty-footer was no joke, recalled Spencer. Rough and heavy work this undoubtedly was, but it still called for both skill and nerve from those engaged on a task which has long (thankfully, some might say) disappeared.

Burnham waterfront between the Crouch Yacht Club and the Maltings Yard in the early years of the century. On the right is the three-masted schooner barge Friendship, *built in 1890 at Sittingbourne and owned by John Smith of Burnham; she was run down and sunk by a steamer in the Humber in 1912.*

Entertainment 4

THE SATURDAY afternoon entertainment high spot for youngsters of the town, particularly boys, was Burnham Electric Kinema. This was in High Street and was later converted into what is now Eastern Electricity showrooms. It was here, after first loading ourselves at Lewsley's greengrocer's shop opposite with what peanuts (twopence per pint) or pomegranates our meagre funds would run to, we watched such nail-biting thrillers as *The Clutching Hand* at the time when Pearl White was the screen idol.

The more exciting and boisterous parts of these silent films often proved too much for us youngsters sitting on wooden forms only a few feet from the screen, and it was not at all uncommon to see the villain pelted with orange peel or pieces of pomegranate, while the hero could always rely on maximum vociferous encouragement.

I well remember one of the many amusing incidents which occurred during the showing of a particularly action-packed western. The hero and the villain were locked in mortal combat and after the hero had taken quite a severe drubbing he eventually gained the upper hand and was poised to administer the *coup de grâce* when the fight was stopped by the Sheriff. This proved too much for one of the lads in the audience, who, completely carried away, rose to his feet and yelled at the top of his voice, "Let 'em finish it."

The more touching love scenes were played out with a background accompaniment of cat calls and wolf whistles. When the young audience became too unruly the film would be stopped, the lights switched on and the proprietor, Mr Charles Newman (nicknamed Squatty, because of his small stature), standing on a chair at the front of the audience, would give the rowdies a tongue-lashing which invariably ended up with the threat that those who did not behave would be thrown out. In these bursts of sabre-rattling he was always backed by his henchman Stan Tunbridge, whose twin brother John was the projectionist, electrician and engineer. Stan it was who, with a hand syringe, used to walk up the single central aisle spraying the audience with a rather pleasant smelling disinfectant.

The price we paid for admission to all this fun was twopence. On leaving school, with our new found affluence—the wage for a school leaver was in the region of six or seven shillings per week—we were allowed by our parents to attend the evening performances and could afford to sit in the sixpenny "padded" seats. The older lads, accompanied by their girl friends and intent on creating an impression, would spring the extra threepence and sit in the top-price ninepenny seats, which were on the raised part of the auditorium farthest from the screen. At these evening performances some of the teenagers were accompanied by their parents, some of whom, through no fault of their own, were unable to read the captions flashed on to the screen, which seldom remained long enough to be read in their entirety. It was the task of the youngsters to read these captions aloud to their parents.

The Kinema had a side exit into a wide entrance into High Street between the Temperance Hotel (now a yacht designer's office) and Mr Fred Hawkins' coal office (now a fish shop). By this access the engine room housing the gas engine which provided light and power for the Kinema could be reached, and on one occasion a lad who had been barred from the Kinema because of misbehaviour gave vent to his annoyance by sneaking up before the engine was

The cast of HMS Pinafore, presented by Burnham Operatic Society at the Public Hall around the turn of the century. Among the "extras" are the local Coastguards, in their blue naval uniform.

"Opening Sunday for Bingo!" says the blackboard, but the Rio Cinema was still showing films during the week when this photograph was taken.

started for the evening performance and ramming a tennis ball down the exhaust pipe. It was some time and many curses later that it was discovered why the engine could not be started.

During the running of the films musical accompaniment was provided by a pianist, who, seated near the screen, would take her cue from the pictures being shown and play appropriate music.

Apart from the cinema, entertainment consisted in the main of smoking concerts, social evenings, dances and whist drives. These were usually staged in St Mary's Hall and later in Coronation Hall (a corrugated iron building erected by Mr John Hawkes and now Tucker Brown's boatbuilding shed) and Queen's Hall, which was in Queens Road. Queens Hall, also a corrugated iron building, was formerly in New Road and was used during the First World War by the Red Cross as a hospital for wounded servicemen. It was subsequently purchased by Mr Robert Leslie and erected on its Queens Road site primarily for use by the Burnham Scouts and Burnham Ramblers, to whom he later gave the hall. The programme at these social evenings and smoking concerts consisted of vocal items, monologues and instrumental items well laced with comedy—all by local artistes. Occasionally the changes were rung when the local branch of the British Legion staged a boxing tournament in the Coronation Hall and in these, too, local lads were the contestants. The dances were quite enjoyable and attended by people of all ages. Music was supplied by local duos (piano and drums) or trios (piano, drums and violin).

In the first half of the century Burnham had several brass bands. Residents spent many a pleasant evening listening to the Burnham Town Band (conducted by Mr Trussell) playing in the bandstand on the Quay in the open space in front of the Anchor Hotel. Whether or not the band dispersed because of the 1914–18 war I cannot say, but it was a good many years later, long after the bandstand had been removed, that the Mildmay Ironworks Band was formed under the baton of "Yorkie" Jackson. This was quite an accomplished band, which functioned for a good many years before being disbanded. Its practice nights were held in the cricket pavilion on Mildmay Ironworks sports field (now Mariners Reach).

For many years on Sundays the Salvation Army Band played hymns in various parts of the town, with good vocal backing by the lady members, who also took the collecting boxes round. A regular and popular Saturday evening pitch was in the High Street opposite the Shore Road junction, busy with people from the marshes and other outlying parts who had come into town to shop. Shore Road corner was a recognized spot where both men and youths with time on their hands would congregate to idle the hours away. Other "loafers," corners were the corner of Crouch Road and Station Road and at the junction of Devonshire Road and Station Road. The latter was invariably crowded on Saturday evenings during the football season. Without either radio or

The Salvation Army hall, to the rear of Warners Hall in High Street, was used by the Salvation Army band on practice nights. The hall was demolished in 1984, soon after this photograph was taken.

television punters had to wait for the arrival by train of the evening paper by which to check whether or not their selections on the betting slips had been right. These betting slips were issued by a local bookie—the names of Vernons or Littlewoods meant nothing at that time.

The Salvation Army headquarters, where the band practised and where they held a Sunday School, was at the rear of Warners Hall in the High Street in a hut loaned free of charge by the owner, businessman Alfred Newman, who was the owner of the Public Hall (later Burnham Electric Kinema). The Salvation Army Citadel on the Brickwall Close–Station Road corner came many years later.

When as youngsters we wanted a day out during school holidays, we would cycle to Creeksea Ferry and ring the bell to summon the boatman from the other side of the river. With our bikes laid in a pile across the stern he would row us over and we would then cycle through Canewdon and Rochford to Southend for the day. Of course there was very little traffic apart from horse-drawn farm vehicles on the road to Southend and the town itself was much quieter. On one occasion when we were there it turned out to be a showery day and we had the High Street to ourselves. Later on in life, when we had left school—usually at the age of fourteen or before that if we could get a job—we became more ambitious and used to travel to Southend by train. The return fare from

Burnham Salvation Army band, which for many years attracted a sizable crowd in High Street when it played there on Saturday evenings.

Burnham on Saturdays was 1s 10d. We used to save up until we had ten shillings and then decide on a day in Southend. This sum would cover the rail fare, admission to a football match, tea, and a show at the Hippodrome in York Road in the evening.

As children we spent winter evenings indoors playing either draughts, ludo or cards with our parents. As a special treat at Christmas my father would get out a clockwork train with carriages. I don't know how far you would get if you tried to amuse a family like this today.

The arrival of a circus was always a great occasion for the youngsters, the free-running circus ponies—usually piebalds and skewbalds—and the horse-drawn cages containing the tigers, bears, and lions being something not to be missed. Another visitor to the town always sure of a welcome from youngsters was the organ grinder, whose barrel organ had a monkey sitting on top holding a tin mug into which it was a great thrill to drop the odd copper cajoled from our parents. And how proud we were if allowed to turn the handle of the organ for a brief spell! Others who made periodic tours of the town were the scissor grinder with his foot-operated contraption of somewhat "Heath Robinson" appearance, and the muffin man with his tray piled high with his wares

To celebrate the ending of the First World War Burnham children were given a tea in High Street, for which they all donned their best clothes.

26

balanced precariously on his head. What a treat these muffins were on a winter evening when toasted and buttered! In the years following the First World War there were frequent visits by travelling musicians—many of them wounded during the war —either singly or in small groups, and an occasional street singer.

More regular callers were the gipsies with their baskets of tin saucepan lids and hand-made clothes pegs and paper flowers. They travelled from town to town in ornate and gaily painted horse-drawn caravans—"with a chimney on top that the smoke comes through", to steal a line from a well-known poem—and when the women called from door to door they more often than not had a baby carried Red Indian fashion on their backs.

The beach near the Pound was a favourite spot for mothers and children alike in the early nineteen-hundreds.

At the turn of the century, by present day standards, there was very little entertainment in the town; small wonder that when the occasion did arise for a bit of fun the lads of the village were inclined to make a meal of it. This comment is qualified by the following extract from the files of the *Burnham Advertiser* of 1901: "At Latchingdon Petty Session fourteen persons were summoned for making a bonfire on the highway at Burnham to the danger and interruption of passengers." At that time it was the custom to celebrate Guy Fawkes day by lighting a bonfire in the High Street and by rolling blazing tar barrels all over the place. Those responsible were not at all choosy as to what they used to keep the blaze going and it was not unknown for the garden "privies" to come to a sudden and ignominious end as fire fodder. At the time of the court case new police officers had been appointed to the district and they tried to stop the practice of lighting a bonfire in the street. The defence was undertaken by Mr L. G. Sandford, a blind solicitor who for many years was a visitor to Burnham, where he owned a yacht. Mr Peter Richmond, called for the defence, said Guy Fawkes day had been celebrated in Burnham in similar fashion for the past sixty or seventy years and there had never been an accident or injury. He also told the court that the police in the past had always kept out of the way. "Not guilty, but don't do it again," was the verdict.

Life in the Home   5

LOOKING back on life in Burnham during the first three or four decades of the century, one cannot help but be impressed by the great extent to which life in the home has changed.

Parents in those days were treated with far greater respect by their offspring than they are today, and good old-fashioned corporal punishment was meted out firmly but fairly to those foolish enough to kick over the traces. But the wrongdoers knew they were only getting their deserts and there was no resentment. Chastisement of youngsters was also carried out by teachers and headmasters, but this did not bring the parents of the chastised children storming to the school in protest. In fact it often worked in reverse: if a parent learned that his child had been "given the stick" he would proceed to give the erring child further punishment to drive the point home that misbehaviour did not pay.

Youngsters certainly had far less freedom and were not allowed out of doors until all hours of the night, as they are today. In summer months it was usually indoors by eight o'clock at night and in the winter months even earlier. And on Saturdays and during school holidays no child was allowed out to play until allotted chores had been satisfactorily completed. Winter nights indoors would be spent playing such games as ludo, draughts, or simple card games, in which both parents (when mother was not too busy patching, darning or ironing) joined.

Bath night came only once a week, on Saturday nights, and with it came clean underclothes, clean night clothes and clean sheets. With large families and the hard work needed on wash days this was quite understandable. And when it came to bathing it must be remembered that nicely heated tiled bathrooms were unknown in the great majority of houses in those days. One washed in a draughty kitchen in a zinc bath. The copper fire would be lit and the largest of the baths used for the weekly washday placed on the kitchen floor, and each of the family bathed in turn. And it was not a case of a fresh lot of water for each. After each bath the "scum" would be skimmed off, a pail of fresh boiling water from the copper put in and it was ready for the next. I was one of a family of seven and can vouch for the fact that by the time the last in line took his bath the water was getting a bit thick.

Over the years the lot of the housewife has certainly changed for

Opposite page: *The staff of A. T. Wilson, upholsterer, cabinet maker and blind maker, are joined by some of the seafaring fraternity on the Quay soon after the turn of the century. A sign in Wilson's window advertises "Yacht cushions made on the premises".*

the better, due in the main to the gadgets which modern science has brought. The drudgery has been taken out of wash day, which in those days was a major operation. First the copper fire had to be lit and kept stoked up, and soda and a grated bar of soap was added to the water—there were no detergents or fancy washing powders. The washing was boiled: "whites" first and "coloureds" later, after they had first been laboriously hand washed on a rubbing board. When the washing had been boiled it was lifted out with a copper-stick—the use of tongs came many years later with the introduction of washing machines—and placed on the upturned copper lid to drain until cool enough to be handled and put through a hand-operated wooden-rollered wringer, which played havoc with all but the linen buttons then much in use. After rinsing in a bath of "blue" water the "whites" were again put through the wringer and then hung out to dry. Spin dryers, drying cabinets and drip-dry articles were luxuries to be enjoyed by later generations. Incidentally, the "blue bag" with which the water was tinted was widely used as an antidote to the stings of wasps, the nests of which seemed far more common than they are today. If a youngster was seen well daubed with blue it was a fairly safe bet that he had stirred up a wasps' nest and stayed too close to the scene for too long.

When the washing was dry and folded it was ready for ironing, but electric and steam irons were inventions of the future; irons in those days were far more primitive, consisting of a silver-plated shield in which the iron was fixed after being heated on an open fire or gas ring.

When I was a child our parents had none of the labour-saving mod. cons. and everything had to be done by hand—and this was in the days of large families. Yet strangely life then seemed far more leisurely. There was time to stand and stare and time for a neighbourly natter. Today, with her smaller family and every modern labour-saving device to hand, mothers seem to be always rushing around with never a moment to spare. I must admit, however, that in the days of my youth the lot of the housewife was lightened to a degree by the fact that tradesmen would call at the door for orders, which they would also deliver. Milk was delivered not in bottles, but from a can taken round from door to door by the milkman. The milk was ladled from the can into the customer's jug by long-handled measures which hung inside the can.

My chores as a child included such tasks as chopping wood ready to stoke the copper fire with on Monday mornings and cleaning the table knives—a tedious job done on a knife board, a leather-faced board about two feet long and five inches wide, using a brown powder known as "Wellington's Knife Powder". Other jobs included cleaning cutlery with "Bluebell", step whitening and boot

Above: Wash day was a major operation before the advent of washing machines and detergents.

A typical baker's roundsman, Len Clark, who spent his whole life in the bakery trade. A handcart was used in the town, but for deliveries to marsh farms and other houses in outlying areas a horse and cart was needed.

and shoe cleaning. Step whitening is something one does not see done today. After the step had been scrubbed clean and while still wet a whitening block was rubbed over it, which when dry left the step a gleaming white. And cleaning shoes was not the simple job it is today. We used boot blacking, a solid lump in a flat tin, on which we used to put either a little water or spit—a thirsty job with several pairs of boots and shoes to clean. One chore I really enjoyed was delivering parcels on Saturday mornings, particularly if they were to one of the marsh farm houses. For this task I was allowed to use the family bike—a real treat was this—and on the return journey I was able to indulge in a spot of "bird nesting".

When our compulsory chores were complete—and not until—it was either down to the river for a bathing session or away to the fields to play, and our parents would see no more of us until meal times came round. The departing threat that nothing would be saved for us if we were not home by mealtime usually had the desired effect. Parents did not make idle threats, as we sometimes learnt to our cost.

Nowadays, when many young mothers have to seek employment, which leaves them little time to prepare meals, it is perhaps quite understandable that "quick food" such as beefburgers, frozen

31

Below: *The town's 30,000-gallon water tower nearing completion in 1910. This tower, in Southminster Road immediately north of St Peter's School, replaced the old brick-built Jubilee tower which had stood on the same site.*

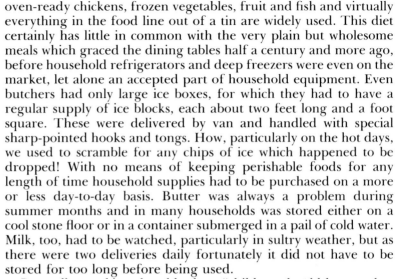

oven-ready chickens, frozen vegetables, fruit and fish and virtually everything in the food line out of a tin are widely used. This diet certainly has little in common with the very plain but wholesome meals which graced the dining tables half a century and more ago, before household refrigerators and deep freezers were even on the market, let alone an accepted part of household equipment. Even butchers had only large ice boxes, for which they had to have a regular supply of ice blocks, each about two feet long and a foot square. These were delivered by van and handled with special sharp-pointed hooks and tongs. How, particularly on the hot days, we used to scramble for any chips of ice which happened to be dropped! With no means of keeping perishable foods for any length of time household supplies had to be purchased on a more or less day-to-day basis. Butter was always a problem during summer months and in many households was stored either on a cool stone floor or in a container submerged in a pail of cold water. Milk, too, had to be watched, particularly in sultry weather, but as there were two deliveries daily fortunately it did not have to be stored for too long before being used.

Generally speaking the old adage "children should be seen but not heard" was put into practice to a far greater extent in my young days than it is today, and there was definitely no talking at the meal table. And as youngsters our plates had to be cleared before we were allowed to leave the table, whether we liked the food or not. If we tried to get out of eating something not to our liking, we were promptly told by our parents, "If you don't like it, lump it," but the meaning of that expression I never understood. On the occasions when there was barely enough meat to go round mother would serve the pudding, probably a huge currant duff, as the first course, telling us youngsters that those who ate the most pudding would have the most meat. But of course by the time we had packed ourselves with pudding we had little appetite left for meat. A favourite for tea with us as youngsters was beef dripping on toast—something one seldom sees on the table these days; how well I remember how we used to scrape down for the tasty brown jelly which had settled in the bottom of the basin.

In the early part of the century many folk, by necessity, lived far more frugally than they do today. Little was wasted; even the burnt scraps left after pieces of fat meat had been melted down were cut into small pieces and put in a cake mixture to end up as scrap cakes, a long-forgotten dainty.

These were the days of large families—anything from six to fifteen, or even more, was the rule rather than the exception. In those days people were not so advanced as today in the field of contraception, and with no radio, no television and many unable to read, there was little left, it seems, to sit up at night for, and the

A group of Burnham worthies in front of the Burnham Yacht Club in 1910, before the club had been granted the "Royal" prefix. Jutting out from the sea wall is an oyster pit; the bandstand in front of the Anchor Hotel can be seen in the background.

large families were a direct result of the long hours spent in bed. Many Burnham men were then employed in the oyster industry and I have heard it said by a Burnham "oldster" that the size of a man's family could be judged by the quantity of oyster shells on his garden path, which speaks volumes for the aphrodisiac properties contained in this aristocrat of the bivalves.

It was a recognized thing for clothes when outgrown by one member of the family to be patched, darned and washed and handed down to the next younger. Having had an older brother I well remember this. The only time I had new clothes, it seems, apart from "Sunday suits" was when my father, a draper in the town, gave me the doubtful privilege and pleasure of wearing up some article of boy's clothing which he had had in stock so long it had become outdated and would not sell. This meant I was wearing, years after it was out of fashion, a Norfolk suit with button-at-the-knee trousers. Another "non-seller" I well remember having to wear for school was a pair of wooden-soled clogs—oh how they echoed in the tile-floored porches at the school! But this I did not mind too much. My real "beef" was that they would not make sparks on the pavement as did the hobnailed boots worn by my school pals.

Very few youngsters could boast owning a cycle and practically every journey was made on foot. Today I often indulge in a silent chuckle when I hear the "kids I knew at school", now aiming at the social ladder, declare (in quite a different tone from that they used when kids) that they do not know how they could possibly manage without their car! How short is their memory.

To help the family purse many mothers made their children's clothes and their husbands' shirts, the material being selected on wearing quality rather than comfort. And how rough, until they had been washed several times, were the sheets made up from unbleached sheeting, which was sold by the yard. These were an oatmeal colour when first made, but gradually became whiter through repeated washing.

Fuel, too, even though coal was two shillings and less per hundredweight, was also a problem for the less well-off. A common

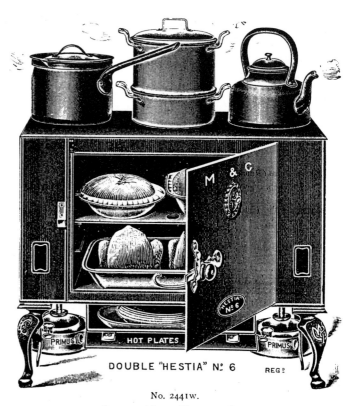

This oven, illustrated in a catalogue issued in 1912, was "specially constructed for large families". The price of 45 shillings (£2.25) would then have represented a considerable investment for many Burnham households.

No. 2441w.

For use with two No. 2425w Stoves.

This Oven has been specially constructed for large families on the same principle as No. 2424w, excepting that two stoves are necessary (one at each end), the plate warmer being at the bottom. There are 3 pot holes at top, and several vessels can be kept boiling. Inside measurements 15 in. deep, 12½ in. high, 18 in. long.

Price **45/-** (with baking pan 17 in. × 12 in.).

sight was of women collecting a bob's worth of coal from the Wharf in a perambulator, or walking the fields and hedgerows in search of wood. Wild rabbits, which were quite plentiful, featured prominently on the menu of most families; at from sixpence to ninepence each they provided a good cheap meal. Most of the eggs, too, came from "backyard hens"—there were not many families without them—and "gleaning" (picking up the ears of corn after the harvest had been gathered in) provided much of the food with which these hens were fed.

As children we used various means to supplement the pocket money given us by our parents (usually a penny a week). During the school holidays we did pea-picking (some schools had a special early short holiday for this) and fruit-picking—raspberries and blackcurrants. As children we were not allowed in the strawberry field, and as it was such a tedious task not many youngsters attempted blackcurrant-picking. It certainly called for a brave heart to collect a half-bushel basket—they seemed enormous to us youngsters, who usually picked in pairs and shared the loot.

Collecting scrap metal and bones during the 1914–18 war also earned us the odd copper or two. We sold them to a Mr Cole, a rag and bone merchant who made a weekly visit to Burnham from Maldon, making his Burnham base at the Welcome Sailor's yard, where he stabled his horse. Bones and scrap metal were bought by weight, and to make our collection register a little extra on the "stilliards"—steelyards or balances—it was common practice to first carefully pack all hollow bones with earth. During the war years we were allowed certain afternoons off from school to go blackberry-picking. The fruit we gathered was taken to school next morning, weighed and sent away in large tub-like containers to be made into jam for the Forces, which leads us to believe that despite the well-known Army song so popular with the troops, they did occasionally have a change from the much maligned "plum and apple jam". So far as I can remember the price we were paid was threepence a pound. On one occasion, when it was my turn to use the family bicycle, I decided to ride to Mayland, where I thought perhaps blackberries might be more plentiful, but when the local lads caught me poaching on what they considered their preserve, I had reluctantly to beat a hasty and ignominious retreat, being given a good send-off with a shower of stones grabbed from the roadside.

Beanfeast parties—an expression seldom heard these days, and of which I do not know the origin—were always good for the odd copper, wheedled from the coach trippers in exchange for bunches of fragrant purple orchids which in those days grew in great abundance in several fields near the Cliffs. We also bunched up and sold watercress, for which we had to make the long trek to the Goldsand Bridges ditches. These outlying districts, particularly the marshes, were our stamping ground, and woe betide those who ventured there without full knowledge of the exact location of every plank bridging the marsh "fleets" in case the farmer or his men gave chase. In the Dammer Wick, Newman's Farm and Hammocks Shed area the man to be feared was the Dammer Wick Farm bailiff, a bearded giant by the name of Woodley whom we treated with great respect; we were always very careful to give him a wide berth; in the Creeksea or Hungerdowns area the man to be avoided was gamekeeper Sam Britain.

Working for a weekly wage of six shillings when I took a regular job after leaving school at the age of fifteen (I had part-time work for twelve months before this), I was never very flush after paying my dues and in common with other lads always looking for an opportunity to make an odd copper. I was able to increase my income by threepence each week when I delivered the *Burnham Advertiser* for sale in the Southminster, Bradwell and Tillingham area to the Southminster newsagent, a local football referee known as Gunner Nunn, who earned the reputation of being the only man who could control a match without moving outside the centre circle. I did this by drawing the permitted sixpence for the return train journey and taking a single fare, walking home across country by way of Ratsborough Farm, Stoneyhills, Romans Farm and the Iron Bridge.

Gaff-rigged open pleasure boats at the Town Steps, seen in a postcard of about 1912.

A quite reliable source of income, for which there was keen competition amongst the lads, was during the yachting season. Lads would turn up at the various landing places—Petticrow's Hard, The Town Hard or Coronation Hard—and when the

*A group of fishermen,
and boys with a toy
sailing yacht, gathered at
the Town Steps in the
eighteen-nineties.*

yachtsmen rowed ashore they would be greeted by cries from the boys of "mind your boat, sir"? It was the task of the lad chosen to keep the dinghy afloat and perhaps do a spot of baling and mopping while the owner completed his business ashore. On his return the lad would be tipped, sometimes quite generously; usually the reward was a "tanner" or a "bob". If he was fortunate he might be able to pick up a little bonus while the owner was ashore by "putting afloat" another yacht owner whose craft was moored on the anchorage.

Then there was the eternal search for discarded returnable mineral water or beer bottles, with which I have known yachtsmen to tip the lad that minded his boat. These bottles were returned to any of the shops or pubs that happened to sell these drinks, and the deposit on the bottles, usually a penny or twopence, was collected. Game, mainly partridges and hares, was plentiful in those days—pheasants were rare—and shooting parties were quite common. Often three or four "bob" could be earned for a day's "beating".

By today's standards the amount of money we were able to pick up seems ridiculously small, but not so puny when compared with the wages of the time. With four shillings (forty-eight pence in those days) one could purchase eight fish and chip meals (a fourpenny piece of fish and twopence-worth of chips) which were on a par with those for which we now pay more than a pound.

During the First World War various methods were used to boost the sale of War Savings Certificates (purchase price 15s 6d, maturing in five years to a withdrawal value of £1). Sixpenny savings stamps were sold in the schools. On one occasion a very low-flying aeroplane passed over the town dropping leaflets advertising Savings Certificates, and word got round—whether it was true or not nobody ever seemed to know—that among these leaflets there was a Savings Certificate. I well remember with a bunch of other lads following a cluster of these leaflets as they fluttered slowly down to earth, eventually (now well scattered) landing on fields on Cherry Gardens Farm, then farmed by a Mr Horrobin. We carefully retrieved every leaflet in sight but no certificate was to be found among them. I expect there are some of us bunch of lads will die wondering whether or not we were conned.

Church Road had a distinctly rural aspect in the early nineteen-hundreds.

Sunday Observance   6

AN EXTRACT from a copy of the *Burnham Review* dated 1899 gives some indication of the almost unbelievable changes which the passing years have brought in the public attitude to Sunday observance. Preaching to a full congregation, Burnham Baptist Minister the Reverend C. D. Gooding asked his congregation to abstain from purchasing the publications of firms which issued Sunday editions of their newspapers. He said he believed that if Christian people throughout the country adopted the same line they would in a few weeks be successful in stopping the sale of Sunday editions by those firms who were trying to desecrate the Sabbath Day. These brave words must have had some effect; at their next meeting the committee of Burnham Reading Room resolved that the *Daily Mail* be excluded from the list of papers taken by them because there was a Sunday edition of that paper.

For youngsters in the days of my youth Sundays meant morning and afternoon attendance at the church of their parents' choice and an afternoon or evening (dependent on the time of the year) family country walk. "Sunday" clothes were worn throughout the day; all games, both outdoor and indoor, were forbidden; and to ensure that Sundays became a rest day in the widest sense, there was no cooking.

A perusal of a publication of the early 1900s—the *Dengie Hundred Free Churchman*, to which all the Free Churches in the Dengie Hundred contributed—makes it quite plain that over the past eighty years there has been quite an easing off in the opposition to drink. These old magazines make many references to Temperance Unions and Bands of Hope. I well remember that as a child I was a member of the Band of Hope run in connection with the Congregational Church and signed a pledge promising to abstain from all intoxicating drinks—a vow which in later life I am ashamed to say proved too much for me. I well remember once being given a sharp reminder of my earlier vow. I was enjoying a pint at the bar of the Royal Corinthian Yacht Club on the occasion of the local club's annual dinner, which I was "covering", when I was spotted by my former Band of Hope leader, Mrs Nessie Tucker, who enquired in a voice that all could hear: "Is that one of my little Band of Hope boys I see drinking at the bar?" I could have crawled under a snake's belly with an umbrella up!

I remember arriving early with three other lads for a Band of Hope meeting, and taking with us a "Frank" heron, which had been shot and left lying on the saltings by Jubal Hawkes, whose grandson, Fred Lester, was one of our party. As we paraded the hapless bird round the meeting room, with its long legs, neck and wings fully extended, we were caught in the act by the caretaker, a Mrs Tracey, a likable old soul who obviously did not approve of our idea of a joke. Looking absolutely flabbergasted, she exclaimed with utter disgust: "Band of Hope! You're more like a band of devils!"

St Mary's Church took the place of an earlier building in the fourteenth century; at the beginning of this century it stood more isolated than it is today.

In those days drunkenness was far more prevalent among grown men than it is now and drink was the cause of a good deal of hardship. Any of Burnham's older residents will recall families which were kept poorly clad and underfed because of the drinking habits of the father of the household. The majority of the cases heard in the local magistrates' courts concerned drunkenness and poaching.

Opposition to drink was also strong in nearby Southminster, as

the following extract from the *Burnham Advertiser* files of 1913 shows:

> At Southminster licensing sessions the magistrates heard in open court an application for the renewal of the licence of the Kings Head, Southminster.
>
> Supt. Smith told the Court that the population of Southminster was 1,567 and there were in the parish six full licences and the nearest licensed house to the Kings Head was the White Hart, which was forty yards distant.
>
> Rev. E. H. Jones, opposing the application, said he thought there were too many licences in the district. His business, he said, was to extend the Kingdom of God and the drink trade seriously interfered with his business. He read a letter from Rev. G. T. Ennals, Baptist minister of Southminster, supporting the objection.
>
> Inspection of the petition presented by Rev. Ennals showed that some of the signatures were repeated seven times and a number three or four times.
>
> The bench renewed the licence.

At the turn of the century there were at least four nonconformist churches in Burnham, two in Althorne and Tillingham and one at Bradwell, which is far more than there are today. Until 1946, when it was destroyed by fire, Burnham Congregational Church stood at the junction of High Street and Chapel Road, and the only buildings between that and the Baptist Church were Cupola House (later council offices), the two brick cottages next door, a small workshop in which Mr "Stivvy" Argent produced clinker-built dinghies, and an old cottage, set well back from the road, which was the home of Mr William King, founder of the boatbuilding firm that still bears his name. Next to the cottage came the large garden of West House, which was enclosed by a brick wall surmounted by ornate iron railings and stretched as far as the Baptist Church.

It was in Belvedere Road, on a site now occupied by the bungalow next to the Victoria Inn, that the Strict Baptist Chapel stood, and here it was that the Reverend Buck held forth to his congregation, which—in the days of my youth at least—could have been counted on one hand and which invariably included Tommy Taylor (a great character well known for his sporting activities) and his sister Bertha. To the best of my knowledge the chapel ceased to function about the same time as did the Catholic Apostolic Church, which was in Providence next to the Queen's Head, then dubbed by locals the "Smiling Lady", because, presumably, of the landlady's grim countenance. The old chapel building is now used as a factory.

Who the minister was in its heyday I do not know, but I do recall that regular attenders were Mr George Gould (who was responsible for the erection of many houses in the town, including some of the earlier council houses) and Mr John Hawkes, who was for many

Burnham Primitive Methodist Chapel in Albert Road was irreverently dubbed "The Six of Diamonds" because of the pattern in the brickwork. It closed in the mid-eighties and became the workshop of a local craftsman.

years proprietor of the Golden Boot Stores, which was in High Street opposite the Constitutional Club. In his younger days he took an active interest in the affairs of the town and served on the Parish Council, and still found time to do a spot of wildfowling. His prowess in the art of punt gunning was well known and earned him many a big bag of wildfowl in the waters of both the Crouch and the Roach. Much of old John rubbed off on to one of his sons, Henry, who also became a bootmaker—home-made "fencers", boots never heard of today, being his speciality—and an expert with a gun, in addition to which he became quite an authority on bees and the owner of several hives. In my younger days, when a swarm of bees was spotted, the recognized course of action was to inform Henry, who, ignoring protective nets and gloves, and armed only with a skip, would arrive in the evening and remove the swarm with a minimum of bother.

The other nonconformist chapel in the town was the Primitive Methodist in Albert Road, irreverently dubbed the "Six of Diamonds" because of the pattern worked in the brickwork at the front of the building. Because of falling congregations this old chapel was closed down in the early nineteen-eighties and was later sold to be used for light industrial purposes. When it was first erected the only buildings in Albert Road were the cottages between that and the Queens Road junction. Opposite, where council houses now stand, was an open field.

Before moving in 1972 to its present Marsh Road site, St Mary's School was in High Street in the buildings with the clock tower known as the Endowed School. It was opened in 1859. The clock tower was added in 1877, erected by public subscription to the memory of Laban Sweeting, a local oyster merchant. In the early days of the school boys and girls were taught separately, with a master for the boys and a mistress for the girls' school. It was a condition of employment that the master live rent free in the school house attached to the school. The trustees of Burnham Charities paid to the master and mistress and other teachers (if any) out of the income of the charities such annual salaries as the trustees from time to time determined and the funds of the charities would permit, not exceeding the following annual amounts: for the master, £60; for the mistress £30; for any assistant teacher, £20.

The school was open to all children between the ages of five and fourteen whose parents were residents of the parish of Burnham, so far as accommodation permitted. It was laid down that the secular instruction of each school—the boys' and the girls'—should comprise reading, writing, spelling, English grammar and arithmetic, and that the religious instruction should comprise the Bible and Bible history and that the catechism be taught. The children were required to attend the schools on Sundays and also to attend divine service at the parish church at least once each Sunday unless there were objections from parents on conscientious grounds. The trustees, if they thought fit, could direct that any weekly sum not exceeding twopence a week be paid by each child attending the school, as "head money".

Burnham Endowed School was built in the early eighteen-hundreds. It is seen here before the erection of a clock tower in 1877 in memory of Mr Laban Sweeting, a prominent Burnham oyster merchant.

43

Former Local Traders   7

BEFORE the pre-packed days much foodstuff was delivered to retailers in bulk. Granulated, demerara and soft brown sugar arrived in hessian sacks, and it was the lot of the grocer's boy (girls were not employed in grocery establishments, except as cashiers) to weigh this up in one-pound or two-pound blue sugar bags. Cube sugar was delivered in strong wooden boxes, ideal for making box carts which were used with comparative safety on the roads, there being only the occasional horse-drawn vehicle, and very little motor traffic as not more than a dozen or so people in the town owned cars.

Treacle arrived in large barrels and was decanted by grocers into large enamel jugs, from which it was poured into the basins or jam jars provided by the customers. This strong-tasting commodity was very popular then as a springtime blood purifier. How quickly the news travelled when a barrel of treacle being delivered to a High Street grocery store fell off the railway company's delivery cart in Providence and burst open, discharging its glutinous mass on to the road! As if by magic youngsters arrived from all quarters with either slices of bread to dip into it or with various containers in the hope of scooping some up!

Butter was delivered in large slabs and it was quite something to watch the expertise with which the grocers wielded their butter pats, knocking the butter into pound or half-pound pats, giving a final smack on the top with a special pat which left a pattern. Dates arrived in slabs about two feet long, a foot wide and eighteen inches high. These would probably stand uncovered on the counter for a week or two before they were all sold—something which would not be allowed today on the grounds of hygiene. The whole cheeses had to be skinned before being cut up with a wire with a handle on each end.

Milk, of course, was not delivered in bottles as it is today. The milkmen did their rounds with either a horse-drawn milk float or a specially designed hand cart on which was mounted a large churn fitted with a plunger in the top to keep the contents mixed. From the tap in this churn the milkmen filled a lidded milk can holding probably three gallons and so designed as to have hooked inside it the long-handled pint and half-pint measures with which the milk was measured off into customers' jugs. The price was three-

Opposite page: *The drapery and outfitting shop of Mr William Henry Clarke and the adjoining grocery shop in Station Road gaily decorated for the Coronation of King Edward VII in 1902.*

halfpence per pint, and skimmed milk could be obtained from Hill Farm, and probably other farms, at a penny a pint.

In those days shopkeepers stuck strictly to their own trade, and butchers', grocers' or bakers' shops selling almost anything, and self-service stores, were unheard of. Before the coming of local branches of chain stores and the introduction of self service the town was well served by family concerns whose courtesy and service left little to be desired.

Over the years the population of the town has grown steadily, but strangely we are not nearly so well off for bakeries as we were in the first half of the century. In those days the town could boast no fewer than seven bakeries, and fresh bread—still warm, in fact—was delivered daily. These bakeries were in Devonshire Road, owned by Mr Joyce, whose retail shop was formerly in Station Road and later in Devonshire Road where the Employment Exchange now is; Mr Taylor's in Alpha Road, later an undertaker's establishment; Newtown Bakery in Crouch Road, owned first by Mr Crix and later by Mr Bill Whife, who had previously taken over Mr Taylor's business, then subsequently, until it was closed down in 1972, by Mr David Patten; Hillside Bakery, at the Queens Road–Station Road junction, owned by Mr Osborne and later by Mr Welch; Smith's Bakery in Station Road opposite the Baptist Church, the premises later used in turn as a wireless and music shop and a butcher's shop before being returned to their original use; Dilliway's (Crouch Bakery) in High Street on the Providence––High Street junction; and Mr Elijah Woolf's bakery in Providence, later owned by one of his sons, and subsequently, until it closed down, by Mr Upson.

Nowadays, when a public announcement such as an unexpected cut in the gas or water supply is to be made, a car or van carrying a public address system makes a round of the town. But in the days of my youth this was not such a simple matter and the news had to be made known by means of the town crier. Perhaps best remembered is Billy Sweeting, nicknamed "Cat", who, armed with his huge handbell and mounted on his tricycle, would ride round the town, stopping at vantage points—usually street corners—to deliver his message. This always started with "O yez, O yez, O yez," and ended with "God save the King." His fee for this lung-testing task was half a crown. In the mornings he forsook his bell for a basket to hawk cakes for Mr Dilliway, always calling at the boatyards around lunchtime. And how good the cakes and buns were in those days—particularly the Chelsea buns with their crisp sugary tops, and the spicy hot cross buns! One might say that this is a case of "Trees are never so tall as in one's youth, landscapes never so grand," but I don't think it is.

The town was also far better served by "snobs", or cobblers, in earlier days than it is today. Mr Bill Cooper operated from premises in Providence; Mr William Wright, whose son Wilfred later succeeded him, had a shoe shop and boot repair business in Station Road opposite St Mary's Hall; Mr Stan Clark had a lock-up shop in Queens Road; Mr Nicholls, a man with malformed feet, had a lock-up shop in Station Road which later became a florist's. These premises have long since been demolished. Others in the trade were Mr Salmons, a man with a wooden leg, whose premises were in High Street next to the Star Hotel, Mr Murrell, whose workshop in Shore Road is now an antiques shop, and Mr John Hawkes whose premises were the Golden Boot Store, one of the parade of shops in High Street between Shore Road and Doctors Lane. In addition several people did shoe repairing as a sideline. These included Mr William Robinson, a postman, who lived in Queens Road.

With horse-drawn vehicles still widely used, it is perhaps not surprising that there was a saddler and harness maker operating in the town. He was Mr Howard Bull, whose premises were in High Street. It follows, too, that there were wheelwrights' and black-

Two old cottages on the corner of High Street and Ship Road, one of which served as a chemist's and druggist's shop. They were later demolished and replaced by another chemist's shop, occupied in turn by Mr J. Watts and Mr H. Tebbutt. The cottage on extreme right has been modernized and is still standing.

smiths' establishments. These were in Marsh Road on a site taken over several years ago for residential development; they were managed by the brothers Arthur and Tom Flick, who lived in the house adjoining with their sister Kate. Most of the farm horses were shod there, the shoesmith for many years being Mr Joe Wagstaff.

There was also a smithy in High Street about midway between Doctors Lane and Shore Road. The proprietor was Mr "Bunny" Harris. He was quite a character, short in patience, particularly with lads who ventured too close when he was busy: they either received a tongue-lashing or had a missile hurled at them for their temerity.

The town's corn and seed merchant was Mr Alfred Hawkins, whose premises in High Street, opposite Warners Hall, were later converted into private residences. His son of the same name started and carried on, until his untimely death, a similar business in Station Road, and his father's brother Fred was one of the town's three coal merchants. The others were Mr A. J. Inch and Mr Arthur Hopgood, both with premises in Devonshire Road. Mr Inch's yard adjoined Burnham County Primary School, which in those days children attended usually until they were fourteen, unless they had jobs to go to before that age. Mr Hawkins housed his coal carts and stabled his horses in Lilian Road, next to its junction with Alpha Road, and in Doctors Lane, in buildings which

Horse-drawn vehicles were available in Burnham for weddings and funerals and for conveying passengers to and from the railway station before the turn of the century. During the summer an open landau was available for visitors wishing to take a drive in the surrounding countryside.

*King and Hines in High
Street used to describe
themselves as yacht
furnishers as well as
ironmongers. The garden
of West House can be
seen on the right.*

were demolished many years ago. These buildings were at the rear
of a public shelter and council depot, and it was here that the fire
engine was housed and where the mortuary was situated. The site
is now occupied by public lavatories.

Several traders daily hawked greengrocery round the town,
some with hand trucks and others using horse-drawn vehicles.
There was also a stout old bowler-hatted gentleman known as
Tubby Williams, who travelled round the district with a huge pack
on his back hawking, I believe, men's clothing. It was the practice,
too, for grocers and butchers to call on their customers for orders,
and no charge was made for delivery, which, of course, was made
in the outlying district by horse-drawn vehicles.

Local traders also supplied Foulness Island, the goods, mainly
groceries and meat, being transported to the island by the Harvey
Brothers in their pleasure sailing boats every Friday morning.
Being a pal of the son of one of the boat owners I was fortunate
enough to be allowed to acccompany my friend on many of these
trips during school holidays, and how we enjoyed them. But how
long and never ending seemed the dusty cart track we had to walk
after disembarking in the Roach—not the easiest of tasks when the
tide was at low ebb—to deliver our load at the island's inn, which
was near the church. With the goods delivered there was a respite
during which the crew enjoyed a beer at the pub while my pal and I
explored before making the long trek back to the boat. While
serving his apprenticeship as a draper and outfitter with a local
establishment my father regularly made a round of the island both
to take orders and to deliver goods.

49

This old butcher's shop, with slaughterhouse and coach house at the rear, occupied the site at the corner of High Street and Chapel Road on which Barclay's Bank now stands. Kendall's business was established, according to an old advertisement, early in the eighteen-hundreds; at the time the photograph was taken the proprietor was Mr I. J. Kendall, who can be seen bowler-hatted, holding his steel in his left hand, outside the shop.

There was certainly no dearth of butchers in the town, and each did his own slaughtering. Mr Walter Carter, who was succeeded by his son Harold, had his retail shop in Station Road near the Devonshire Road junction and a slaughterhouse in buildings at the rear of what is now the Post Office, and Mr T. E. Osborn, who was succeeded by his son and later a grandson, had premises with a slaughterhouse at the rear on the Chapel Road–High Street junction on the site now occupied by Barclays Bank. Other local butchers were Mr Blaxill, whose premises were on the Station Road–Queens Road corner, Edward Paynter, whose shop (with slaughterhouse at rear) was on the Station Road–Western Road corner, and which has been a butcher's shop ever since, Webster's in the High Street in the row of shops between the Shore Road and Doctors Lane junctions, and Dick Lipscombe, whose premises were in Station Road near the Crouch Road junction. Folk were far less particular about hygiene than they are today. One Saturday afternoon I was with the late Sidney Read in the backyard of his father's grocery/butchery/greengrocery shop (now Rumble's hair-dressing salon) when down the garden path came Sidney James

50

Read senior and the employee of one of the local butchers dragging by its back legs a pig which they had slaughtered in Tom Nethercoat's barn on the field at the back (now Brickwall Close). The carcase of the hapless animal was manoeuvred through the kitchen door and plunged into the domestic bath containing very hot water, and the scraping off of the bristles commenced. I did not stay to see what happened next but I suspect that jointing (carried out on the kitchen table) followed and that eventually the meat was sold over the counter.

Sidney James was certainly a character. At one time he took up chimney sweeping, and the story has been told that on one occasion he was sweeping the chimney of a house in Granville Terrace and asked a lad to let him know when the brush showed out of the chimney pot. Tired of waiting, the lad disappeared, and Sidney James continued to put on more and more rods. Wondering what had gone wrong, he opened the back door to see what was happening and walked into the brush.

Then there was the occasion when a wild rabbit was being chased in the High Street. As it came past the clock tower and continued on past Bunny Harris's and Webster's butcher's shop (now a fish shop and ladies' hairdressers) Mr Webster captured it, and within minutes it had been gutted and was hanging up for sale in his shop. Who could wish for fresher meat than that?

Before the coming of abattoirs and the days when local butchers turned to purchasing ready-dressed carcases, Burnham butchers obtained the bulk of their meat at Mr Ernest J. Gale's weekly stock sale, held at Southminster on Tuesdays. Here the beasts, prime stock raised mainly on the marshes where grazing land was plentiful, were brought in from the outlying farms and penned before they came under the hammer. With butchers from the whole of the Dengie Hundred and beyond present, bidding was lively and trade brisk.

The sale over, all the bullocks and sheep purchased by Burnham butchers were herded together and driven the three miles to Burnham by an old drover named Billy Bunn. The pigs were transported by specially designed low-slung horse-drawn vehicles covered by a substantial net. During school holidays several of us Burnham lads would walk to Southminster via Stoney Hills and Ratsborough fields, watch the sale of stock and then help old Billy, who after a lengthy session in the nearby Station Arms—which was open all day on market days—was not always quite sober, drive the animals to Burnham by road. There was not enough traffic to create a problem, which was perhaps just as well.

Apart from the occasions on which one or more of the animals chose to be awkward the journeys generally proved uneventful, although with the consent of the drover we usually contrived to allow the sheep to stray into Newman's Orchard, immediately north of the railway bridge and now forming part of the Maple Leaf estate, which gave us the opportunity to purloin a few windfalls before driving the animals out again. As we gave our services—for what they were worth—free of charge, this spot of scrumping seemed quite legitimate "perks." Having a fairly intimate knowledge of the orchard, we certainly knew the trees on which grew the choicest fruit.

Cattle and sheep are not seen in the streets of the town today but quite sizeable flocks of sheep used to be driven through the town to graze on the marsh farms, and a herd of dairy cows were driven twice daily from Mill Field, where they grazed, to be milked at Jack Nethercoat's dairy in Silver Road. With tradesmen's, farm and local council vehicles all horse drawn, it was necessary for the brooms used by road sweepers to be fitted with stout metal scrapers.

There were also pork butchers' shops in Lilian Road (proprietor Mr Woods, perhaps better remembered as caretaker of the Devonshire Road School) and in High Street, opposite the Ship

The Railway Hotel was, like much of Burnham, gaily bedecked to celebrate the Coronation in 1902. It has since been renamed the Railway Arms.

52

Hotel (the proprietor Mr Judah Lee, who later opened a butcher's shop in Tillingham).

There were three barbers in the town, but no hair styling centres or blow wave specialists in those down-to-earth days. Mr Powell collapsed and died in his shop in High Street opposite Barclays Bank. John Mellard (his grandson of the same name now runs a hairdressing salon in the town), assisted by his sons, had premises in High Street which were gutted by fire one Saturday night. The most colourful of them all, a lively old character named Jack Overton, traded from premises next door to the Station Road Post Office. In the shop next door his wife sold confectionery and tobacco, and on display in the window was an evil-looking black coil of twist, used mainly as chewing-tobacco, a habit widely indulged in by the working class in those days. At this time cigarettes were fourpence for a packet of ten for the cheaper brands and sixpence for ten for the better makes.

Mr Overton's waiting customers would either listen to his never-ending and often amusing patter or become absorbed in the gory

The Star Hotel in High Street was at one time only one of more than a dozen licensed houses in the town.

53

items recorded in the pink pages of the *Police Gazette*. Background music was provided by the smoke-blackened kettle (for shaving-water) singing merrily on the kitchen range. Shampooing was not Mr Overton's line of country, so no washbasin was fitted. Here a shave cost twopence—I know, because it was here that I had my first shave before I left school—and a haircut (only one "style", close cropped all over except for a fringe in the front) fourpence.

Also in the town were two mineral water manufacturers, the brothers Arthur and Harry Wright and John Bacon. The former had premises on Hillside between the Oyster Smack and what was then the Gas Works site but which now houses Dilliway Court, and Mr Bacon's premises were in Riverside Road. Both firms have long since closed down. The favourite drink produced by the Wright brothers was American cream soda in bottles with a glass marble stopper. These glass stoppers were much sought after for use in marbles games, which were always popular.

Despite the smaller population, Burnham had more public houses at the turn of the century than it has today. These were: White Harte, Anchor, Ship, Star, Railway, Kings Arms (now Constitutional Club), Welcome Sailor, George and Dragon (at Ostend), Oyster Smack, Victoria, Waggon and Horses (a beerhouse at the end of the High Street opposite the Victoria), Queens Head, Rising Sun, Temperance Hotel and a beerhouse known as the Kicking Dicky, which was situated in Marsh Road opposite The Leas estate; this hostelry was flattened when a bomb disposal unit exploded an enemy parachute mine which had landed in the field opposite during the Second World War.

The Kicking Dicky, an old beerhouse in Marsh Road whose correct name has been forgotten. A dicky is a donkey, and many a badly-painted sign showing a horse gained such a nickname.

Local Doctors 8

IN THE early part of the century doctors' services and the medicines they supplied had to be paid for by the patients, but most families had little left to meet a doctor's charges after paying out for essential day-to-day items. This meant that a doctor was not called in until all the home remedies and quack cures had failed. Because of this delay he often found a desperately ill or even a dying patient on his hands—a critical situation which earlier professional attention might well have avoided.

Because of the financial aspect doctors' surgeries in those days were not the crowded waiting places they were immediately before the opening of the Health Centre in Foundry Lane. When anyone did visit the doctor—a visit to the surgery was less expensive than a home visit by the doctor—it was a safe bet that they were really ill. Practically all patients were nursed at home, and to deaden the noise caused by traffic, mainly horse-drawn farm vehicles and tradesmen's carts, all of which had iron-tyred wheels, it was not an uncommon sight to see the road outside the home of a seriously ill person thickly coated with straw.

Doctors in the early part of the century made their rounds on cycles, but later graduated to motor cycles and eventually joined the ranks of the few car owners. One of the town's medicos who never did progress beyond the cycle status was Dr T. D. White, a down-to-earth old character whose surgery was in the High Street at the junction with Doctors Lane. He was a keen cricketer, a prominent playing member for many years of Burnham Cricket Club, whose ground was at Saltcourts—now the Royal Corinthian Yacht Club's boat park. I well remember my visit, when a 15-year-old, to this likable character, whose duty as the town's Medical Officer of Health it was to check, under the Factories Act, that anyone entering industry was medically fit to do so. My examination proved cursory, to say the least, and could not have taken longer than a minute. Having disclosed the reason for my visit and answered in the affirmative to the question "Do you eat, drink, swear and play cricket?" I was asked for my shilling, the fee for the examination, the register was signed, and the examination was over.

Until doctors came under the National Health Service it was common practice for patients to attempt to cure what appeared to be common ailments by patent medicines, some of which were claimed to be the panacea for all ills and ailments from backache to biliousness. These branded products—backache and kidney pills, liver pills, stomach powders and that most wonderful curative of them all, syrup of figs—could be obtained at the many confectionery and tobacconists' shops, not a few of which were merely a front room of a private house.

In a publication of the late eighteen-nineties I came across one or two advertisments for these quack cures. Steedman's soothing powders claimed to relieve feverish heat, prevent fits, convulsions, etc. Braggs' vegetable charcoal was for indigestion, fevers, cholera, liver disorders, sleeplessness, etc. What the etcetera was I shrink from hazarding a guess. And Whelpton's pills were described as the best family medicine and a certain cure for headache and constipation.

Home cures much used were bread poultices for boils and whitlows (a painful swelling at the base of the finger nails seldom heard of today but a common ailment in my childhood), "bluebag" (a cube of Reckitts' blue tied in rag and dipped into the rinsing water to make sheets "whiter than white") or vinegar to take the soreness out of wasp stings, which were very common. "Poker beer" (beer with a hot poker plunged into it) was a sure cure for the common cold, mustard plasters eased lung congestion, and a home-made liniment, some of the ingredients of which were turpentine, egg whites and white vinegar, rubbed gently into the affected parts would ease stiffness or rheumatic pains. In those days many children seemed to suffer from earache, and to prevent this painful ailment many youngsters had their ears permanently stuffed with cotton wool soaked in almond oil. But springtime was the time for the big purge. Mothers, including mine, would then mix up a large basin of flowers of sulphur and treacle and feed a teaspoonful to each of her children before sending them to school each morning. It certainly got results.

When the doctor was called in and minor operations such as the removal of tonsils became necessary a table was prepared in a bedroom at the patient's home and this became the operating theatre. But still, it seems, a good many of us got through to tell the tale.

Not all youngsters came through unscathed from injuries received in school accidents—injuries which now with the aid of such present-day drugs as penicillin would present very few problems. Take, for instance, the case of well-known Burnham-born Norman Richmond. During his school days he fell in the playground, sustaining a minor injury to his leg below the knee. When the wound failed to respond to the usual home treatment medical advice was sought. There followed six weeks of hot

56

The nurses' home in Albert Road, built by public subscription in 1937 and opened by Lady Rayleigh. Following local government reorganization in 1974 the property was sold for conversion into flats.

fomentations—much favoured in those days—applied by the district nurse, who at the time was Nurse Hawkes, a lovable old soul who made her daily rounds, taking confinements and laying out the dead in her stride, and always ready with a comforting word of reassurance or advice. When in spite of this professional treatment the leg worsened somewhat alarmingly, the unfortunate lad was ordered to St Bartholomew's Hospital. But this did not mean, as it would today, a two-hour trip in a comfortable well-sprung ambulance with a competent ambulance attendant accompanying the patient. For his trip to Liverpool Street Norman was transported on an improvised stretcher in the guard's van of a passenger train. On arrival at Liverpool Street Station the patient's eldest brother, a porter at Burnham Station who was taking the lad to hospital, borrowed a station luggage truck from a fellow porter and on this wheeled his young brother to St Bartholomew's Hospital. In hospital the wound failed to respond to six operations and intensive treatment, in which the use of massive quantities of iodine featured prominently, and amputation of the leg at the knee became necessary.

It was quite a performance when as a lad, after a succession of sore throats, it was advised that I should have my tonsils removed. The operation cost two guineas which I had to pay myself out of the money I had managed to save. Our family doctor was Dr Lander, whose residence and surgery was in the High Street next to the Drill Hall. A London throat specialist visited one Sunday, and the surgery became the operating theatre for the day, as several children were to have a similar operation. I walked the three-quarters of a mile to the surgery, and after a short period in the waiting room my turn came. I was stripped to the waist and laid on the operating table, where the anaesthetic was administered by Nurse Hawkes, who covered my mouth and nose with a pad of cotton wool, on to which she dripped chloroform, and told me to breathe deeply and count up to thirty. So far as I can remember I only managed to count up to about twelve before passing out. When I regained consciousness I was back in the waiting room, and when I seemed to be fully recovered I dressed and got up with the intention of walking home. But although the spirit was willing the flesh was still weak, and after I had been violently sick I was taken home by car. This was the first ride in a motor car I had ever had. I was reminded just how things have changed in the matter of minor operations when my son had his tonsils removed. This meant a two-day spell in hospital, and no charge was made.

The trend nowadays is for babies to be born in the maternity wards of hospitals, and with the departure of the former practice of babies being born at home have gone all the old birth customs and superstitions.

When a child was born with its head encased in a caul, this thin membrane was dried and carefully preserved in the belief that whoever possessed it would never drown. Among my mother-in-law's prized possessions was one of these somewhat gruesome keepsakes, which must have been well over eighty years old before it was discarded. When there was a new arrival the custom was for the child's father or grandfather to "cross its palm with silver" to ensure that throughout its life the newborn would never be without money. If a child was born with a birthmark this was attributed to some incident which had occurred to the mother during preg-

Mr H. L. (Len) Tunbridge at the wheel of one of the first cars to be seen in Burnham. It is believed that the owner was Mr Chester Jones, of Church Road. Doctors were among the early car owners, but there were some who never did give up their bicycles.

nancy. Thus a birthmark resembling a spider or a bird, for example, signified that the mother had been frightened by one of these creatures. The more common "strawberry mark" meant, of course, that the mother had eaten too many strawberries.

It was also fondly believed in the days of my youth that a snake's skin worn inside one's hat would keep the wearer free from headaches. Another belief, which crafty bricklayers did their best to ensure was carried out, because this invariably meant a free drink for them, was that beer poured down the chimney when the stack was completed ensured the fire would never smoke.

Other superstitions were that anyone who robbed a robin's nest would break a limb; to see three crows flying together was a sign of death in the family; and bad luck would come to those who opened an umbrella indoors, laid new shoes or boots on the table or brought may-blossom or pussy-willow (always known to us as palm) into the house. Knives laid crossed on the table was a sure sign that strife in the family was to follow.

The past sixty years have certainly brought change in the procedure followed when there is a death in a family. No longer are the blinds of the house of the bereaved family, their relatives and neighbours drawn and left so until after the funeral, nor are the blinds of the houses and shops on the route to the cemetery drawn while the funeral cortège passes. Also gone is the practice of fixing a black board some six inches wide vertically down the window of business premises in which the death of the proprietor has occurred. And no longer do relatives wear deep-mourning clothes or a black band round their arm for a month or more after their bereavement.

The King's Arms in High Street described itself as "The Noted House for Old Mild Ales from Writtle, Essex". For many years it has been the Constitutional Club.

Changes on the Land   9

IN THE agricultural industry in the past half century the horse has been superseded by the tractor. The stirring sight of a horseman expertly handling his plough and pair of massive shaggy-legged shires, which he controlled with mystic utterances obviously so well understood by his trusty pair, is not for modern eyes. Those who, like myself, have nostalgic memories of this once common sight of four or five horsemen and their well-matched pairs at work in one field, with myriads of seagulls in their wake against a backcloth of trees and hedgerows, will mourn the changing scene. Seagulls were particularly abundant when sprats were being ploughed in. These sprats were brought in by the smack-load and off-loaded into waiting tumbrils—high-wheeled smallish open farm carts. The fish were taken from the hold in what must have been bushel baskets and carried along a plank from smack to shore on the shoulders of the unloading gang, whose only protective clothing was a sack draped across their shoulders. Looking back, this seems to have been a criminal waste of good food. It certainly makes one realize just how ruthlessly and with no thought for the future man has plundered the world's natural resources throughout the ages—ultimately to his own detriment.

How good it is to recall the sight of a self-binder drawn by a pair of horses at work in the harvest field! And this early step towards mechanization of the industry certainly brought problems to the farmworkers, who had hitherto required little more than a knowledge of the use of hand tools and an ability to handle horses.

As boys we were allowed in the harvest fields to catch rabbits as they bolted from the ever-diminishing standing crop as the self-binder, with its hot and dusty driver and his pair of fly-plagued horses, their backs usually protected from the persistent pests by pieces of sacking, continued relentlessly on its round leaving rows of sheaves in its wake. When the crop had more than usual "bottom", or weeds, a farmworker walked beside the self-binder. His task was to see that the sheaves were being thrown out properly tied and to clear the machine when it became choked through an excess of weeds or through the crop having "laid" or been flattened by wind and rain. Not surprisingly, stoppages were by no means uncommon, but this was in the days when there was time to stand

A nineteenth-century farmworker, from a photograph taken by pioneer photographer P. H. Emerson.

and stare, and nobody seemed to mind too much if progress was slow. Perhaps this is not to be wondered at when it is remembered that a farmworker's weekly wage was only twenty-five shillings.

By comparison harvesting is a simple process today, the age of the combine harvester. When self-binders were in use the land was always on the stetch, and the width of each cut was half a stetch; nowadays the land is no longer stetched and the present-day monsters move in, cutting and threshing in one process what must be the equivalent of a two-stetch width each cut and discarding the straw, which is usually burnt *in situ*. Laid crops or bad weather fail to delay the operation unduly; if it is found that the grain has an excessive moisture content it is simply treated in the drying-shed—another modern innovation.

In the days of the self-binder, which superseded the gangs of hand reapers, workers armed with scythes would cut a strip round the edges of the field wide enough for the self-binder to work in, the corn they cut being tied into sheaves with twisted straw binders. When the self-binder had done its job the "travers" took over. Their task was to pick up the sheaves and stand them in "stooks" of about ten—four at each side and one at each end. After the crop had been left to dry out the carters came and with their pitchforks loaded the waggons—their "ladders" extending fore and aft—to a great height, and took their load to the stackyard to be stacked. Thatching followed as soon as possible and the fields, with their golden harvest now cleared, were raked with a single-horse hay rake and the rakings used for litter. It was not until this stage that the gleaners were allowed into the fields.

Harvest time was hot and thirsty work, but most farmers kept their workers well supplied with "harvest beer", which could be

Narrow Wheel Hoop Waggon

A waggon of the kind used for much of the carting on the farm, from a nineteenth-century rural encyclopaedia.

bought at sevenpence a gallon (old money!). Later, when "all was safely gathered in", farmers, to show their appreciation of their employees' efforts, would give them a harvest supper. These were great occasions, with a good spread and lashings of beer. Towards the end of the evening, when the drink was beginning to have its effect, there was a session of impromptu entertainment. This was given by the workers themselves and usually took the form of unaccompanied and somewhat ribald vocal solos, community singing and solo dances, with the "fencer", a type of boot favoured by farmworkers, tapping out a resounding tattoo on the hall floor.

It was not until the winter months that the stacks in the stackyard were threshed out. This was carried out by threshing tackle powered by a steam engine and was yet another dusty job. Before a stack was threshed out it was surrounded by fine-mesh wire netting to prevent the escape of any rats or mice which had decided to winter in the stacks. To the layman stacking may seem a fairly straightforward task, but in reality it is an art in itself which needs a great deal of experience. The stacker must first size up the crop and with only his judgement to guide him decide what size the base of the stack must be. As stacking proceeds he must judge at what stage to start to taper to form the sloping top—not an easy task. The accuracy of experienced stackers was almost uncanny and their knowledge stemmed not from agricultural college but from personal experience and advice handed down from earlier generations.

Thatching was also something in which thatchers took a great pride, and a stackyard packed—dangerously close to each other, it seemed, in view of the fire risk—with well-stacked neatly thatched stacks was indeed something of which those responsible had every reason to be proud.

Since my retirement I have been on a conducted tour of a modern marsh farm while harvest was in full swing, and was forcibly reminded just how vast are the changes which have taken place since my youth, not only in methods and machinery but also in the farmworkers themselves. Gone are the farmworkers who spent practically all their working time afoot and were dedicated men—they had to be to tolerate the working conditions which existed at the time. For the horseman it was a long and tiring day, particularly at ploughing time when it was up and away early to walk or cycle to the farm to bring in, feed and groom his horses before harnessing up to start his day behind the plough. A brief break at "beaver" time was followed by the midday break, when the horses were given their nosebags in which they munched and snorted contentedly whilst their master ate his frugal midday meal, often bread and cheese and a raw onion washed down with a bottle of cold tea. I cannot recall ever seeing a Thermos flask in use, but whether or not they were on the market in those days I know not. Although these men could not demand a high wage they were nonetheless generally speaking fine craftsmen for whom I have nothing but admiration.

By comparison the farmworker of today, although equally as proficient as his predecessors, is a man of a quite different breed. He more than likely travels to his work by car and spends a good many of his working hours in the air-conditioned cab (fitted with an all-stations radio) of some powerful and complicated machine which is probably capable of doing the work of a score of farmworkers of the old school. But with such machinery to operate, and if needs be repair, he must be quite strong and have a good knowledge of mechanics. With the greater understanding of soil structure and with the wide diversity of fertilizers and pesticides available, the farm manager must have an intimate knowledge of each field and know which treatment each field must receive if maximum yields are to be maintained.

Regrettably modernization on the farm has seen almost the end of our patchwork countryside with its small fields divided by trees and hedgerows. In its place we have monotonously large fields, to provide which trees and hedgerows, and with them the habitats of wildlife which was so much a part of the country scene, have been sacrificed.

In the past women and boys played their part on the farm, the women on such tasks as rhubarb pulling, "docking" (pulling docks and other large weeds from the standing crops), potato picking, hoeing and fruit picking, while it was a boy's job to do the "scare-crowing"—walking round the fields where grain had been sown making as much noise as possible with their home-made clappers to keep rooks, pigeons and any other predators on the move and away from the fields in their charge.

Huge lorries loaded with two tiers of tightly packed sheep or cattle are not an uncommon sight on our roads today, but in earlier days stock moving was undertaken by drovers, and what a leg-wearying task theirs was.

Charlie Tracey, Burnham's last surviving drover of the old school, was in his early twenties when he became drover in the employ of well-known Burnham farmer and cattle and sheep dealer Mr Frank Stebbing, of Strathmore, Crouch Road. Mr Stebbing farmed West Wick on Burnham Marshes, where he fattened cattle until they were ready for slaughter, and one of Charlie's regular weekly tasks was to drive a batch of around twenty steers to Chelmsford cattle market, which was held on Fridays. Reared in the remoteness of the marshes, these animals were usually a wild-eyed and wilful bunch, and the journeys to market were seldom without incident. Starting his drive on Wednesdays and taking matters steadily, to ensure the cattle were delivered in prime condition, the drover bedded his charges down for the night in a field at Purleigh, taking them next day as far as Danbury, where they spent the night in another hired field. On Friday morning it was an early start and a leisurely drive to market. But Charlie's drives were not all as easy as these weekly trips to Chelmsford.

His most tiring day, he recalled, started by driving a flock of sheep from West Wick to Steeple, where he was picked up by his employer in his Model T Ford car, and returned to West Wick. There he collected three horses, which he took to Chelmsford, arriving too late to catch the last bus and having no alternative but to walk home. He eventually reached Burnham soon after 3 am after spending an hour with a night watchman at Purleigh *en route*. Another occasion well remembered by Charlie was when his employer travelled to Scotland, where he purchased a thousand sheep at half a crown per head. Transported by rail, the huge flock duly arrived at Maldon West station and Charlie claimed that when the last of the flock was being off-loaded at the station the vanguard of the flock had already reached Cups Corner. The flock was driven the three miles to Mundon Hall, where the drover-cum-shepherd, living in an on-site caravan and doing his own catering, spent several months watching over them. The flock was gradually

A typical harvest scene of earlier days, taken on Burnham Marshes around the turn of the century.

sold piecemeal in batches of up to a hundred at prices varying from thirty shillings to £2 per head. Another long haul for Charlie was when he drove five hundred sheep from Canvey Island, then little more than rough grazing ground, to a farm near Terling. He had an assistant for the four-day journey.

The drover employed by Burnham butchers to bring the cattle they bought at Southminster market to slaughterhouses (pigs and sometimes sheep were on occasion delivered by farm carts, the animals secured under a large-meshed rope net) was Billy Bunn, a likable old character with a tell-tale blue-veined nose. After spending more time than he perhaps should have done in the Station Arms (Southminster public houses were allowed to open all day on market days), he was often hardly in a fit state for the job in hand—but somehow he managed. Another drover I can recall who regularly attended Southminster market was named Rich, a lantern-jawed hard looking character who always wore a bowler hat. It was his job to get the cattle into the sale ring, walk them round until the bidding was finished and then drive them out again and bring in the next beast to come under the hammer. I always enjoyed a day at Southminster market.

Change there must be, and change there has been, and in this respect the marshes have certainly not been left behind. Over the past half century their character has been transformed.

As youngsters during the spring months we regularly roamed

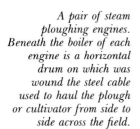

A pair of steam ploughing engines. Beneath the boiler of each engine is a horizontal drum on which was wound the steel cable used to haul the plough or cultivator from side to side across the field.

the marshes in search of plover and moorhen eggs, and as a result we became quite familiar with the location of every footbridge (usually a nine-inch plank with no handrail) and field gate, knowledge which was a must if we were to avoid being nabbed by either the farmer or his "looker". These sorties, made in kind spring weather, with the prospect of being chased adding extra spice, were indeed great stuff. But for me it was not until I was a twelve-year-old, when I first went out with a shooting party to carry some of the "bag", that I was to see the other side of the coin and learn just how bleak, but to me nonetheless appealing, this same marshland could be. This was particularly true when the wind, perhaps bearing a flurry of snow, swept in from the adjoining North Sea, with neither tree nor hedge and only the occasional hay stack to check its rush or to offer shelter.

In those days only a small proportion of the marshland was under the plough and the main use of the rough grassland was as grazing land for cattle, sheep and horses. With its abundance of hares and partridges, and always a chance of wildfowl, the marshes were much sought after by shooting parties and commanded a high price for shooting rights.

The first couple I went with, to walk between the guns and carry the "bag", were two local builders, George Bacon and Edward Read. They were a pair who picked their days, and outings with them were usually uneventful but nonetheless tiring, as at the end of the day it meant a cycle-ride home with progress made difficult by hares and partridges hanging from the handlebars.

By comparison, days with those redoubtable old sportsmen Jack (Pip) Handley, proprietor of the Old Ship Hotel, and Jim Bridge, who at the time was employed at the Star Hotel, were far richer in incident and etched themselves more deeply on my mind. The day invariably opened on a hairy note with a hazardous trip over the deeply pot-holed flint-constructed marsh road in a Model T Ford—which seemed equally draughty with its canvas hood either up or down—with Jack Handley at the wheel. This perhaps sounds safe enough, but when it is known that our driver's eyesight was far from perfect and that the road was bordered for most of its length by a deep ditch, usually well filled, the dangers become more apparent. Just how poor our driver's eyesight really was can be judged from the fact that I was given the seat beside the driver and it was my job to tell him on approach whether or not the many gates which crossed the road were open or shut. If they were shut I had to open them to let the car through. I can still recall old Pip, his steel-rimmed spectacles perched on the end of his purple-veined nose, with head forward, peering intently ahead and asking, as we came dangerously near to a gate: "Is that gate open or shut, boy?"

With our car parked either near farm buildings or beside a

This photograph of the saltings west of the Dandy Stile shows how greatly the saltings have been eroded over the past half-century.

haystack, the day's shoot would begin, and if the party included, as it often did, above average shots, it was a safe bet that I was in for a hard time. Walking for what at times seemed miles, with a couple of huge marsh hares, which at the time seemed to me to be as big as donkeys, slung over each shoulder, and a brace or two of partridges in my hands for good measure, the midday break was, to me at least, very welcome. For me this was a four-bob-a-day job with lunch (a hunk of bread and cheese and a bottle of ginger beer) thrown in and occasionally a bit of bonus in the form of a tip from some of the party, although these seldom came unless the donor had had a particularly good day. On one very cold day, as we took our lunch break huddled out of the wind under a haystack, I must have looked utterly cold and dejected because one of the party handed me a small glass of amber liquid with the comment: "drink this, boy, it will warm the cockles of your heart and put hairs on your chest." How I choked and how my eyes watered—to the great amusement of the party—when the neat whisky hit my throat, but what a pleasing warm glow throughout my numbed body was to follow!

The marshes today, with the tarmac road free from gates and much of the land now under cultivation, are a far different and seemingly less wild place.

When I was a youngster Saturday was a great day for farmworkers and their families living on the marshes and in outlying areas. This was the day when the week's shopping was done and the only time when the farmworkers' wives came into town. The families arrived in various types of horse-drawn farm vehicles or on cycles, and while father had a noggin at the pubs of his choice, mother and children did a round of the shops. Many ended the day with a real treat—a fish and chip supper, which, well salted and dripping with vinegar, would be eaten from its newspaper wrapping on the journey home. This was not a particularly comfortable journey in those days, when the flint road was invariably in a bad state of repair and there were the many gates to hamper progress. These fish and chip suppers were obtained at "Fishy" Adams' shop in Devonshire Road, which was run by an ageing couple whose cleanliness and hygiene was not their strongest point, to say the least.

Never over-flush, these farmworkers seldom missed an opportunity to make an extra shilling or two on the side, and when they came into town they not infrequently brought in a "Sally" or two, as hares were known, a pair of wild ducks, rabbits, perhaps a fowl, or even mushrooms. These would either be sold or bartered for clothes, groceries or a pint or two. My father being a draper in the town, with a big family to feed, was not averse to making a deal in

The Old Ship Hotel, of which Jack (Pip) Handley was proprietor.

this way, and as a result jugged hare sometimes appeared on the table.

Some farmworkers not infrequently changed their employers, and when they moved from one farm to another, often in a distant parish, everything—including furniture, household utensils, children, animals, chickens—was transported in one load on a horse-drawn farm waggon probably borrowed from the new employer.

In my school days children from the marsh farms were conveyed to and from school by a canvas-topped two-horse brake with plank seats. In the winter months, when the journey home was in gathering darkness, oil lamps on the side of the cart were lit. Two of the drivers I remember were "Curly" Wallace and "Cockney" Wallis, the latter quite a character who walked with a distinct limp; he hailed, as his nickname suggests, from the metropolis. Both were employed by Mr Wilfred Newman, of Hall Farm, from whom the horses and brake were hired.

Very few children owned cycles, and the vast majority, a good number of whom lived anything up to two miles outside the town, made the journey to school on foot, carrying their sandwiches in a satchel. School buses were to come much later. There were no school meals for those children who could not get home at midday, and certainly no free school milk. The lofty classrooms were heated by a single open coal fire which provided only a minimum of warmth, unfortunately for those seated at the back of the classroom farthest from the fire. This position, however, had its compensations in that it was well removed from the teacher's eye.

Burnham Council School in Devonshire Road which when completed in 1901 accommodated more than five hundred boys and girls. The garden plots on the left were cultivated by the older boys. All the buildings were demolished in 1989 when the site was sold for redevelopment.

From Fields and   10
Hedgerows

FOR EVER roaming the countryside as youngsters, we became proper little hedgerow urchins and got to know the exact location of every wild plum, crab apple and wild bullace tree, the streams in which grew the best watercress, and the hedgerows from which the greatest quantity and most luscious blackberries could be picked, as well as where to make for when in search of a hockey stick, fishing pole or catapult "scrotch". The selection of one of the latter was not something we took lightly. These were searched out—usually in young growth of ash—when still quite small and painstakingly tied in to form the desired shape and left to grow to the required size, which could mean anything up to a two years' wait. How annoying it was to have a "scrotch" which we had trained and watched taken by some other lad just when it was about ready to meet our own discerning requirements. And how proud we were of our possession when we were fortunate enough to obtain the perfect much-favoured "egg-cup" shaped "scrotch" to become the envy of other lads.

We knew, too, where to go and at what time of the year for either sloes or mushrooms and were familiar with the fields and that part of the railway embankment where wild strawberries grew, and the places where rabbits could be snared without our being caught ourselves. It was the same with the wild purple sweet-smelling orchids, wild marguerites and "bobbing Joans", the name by which we knew bulrushes. Most lads took pride in their collection of birds' eggs, and when any particular kind of egg was sought we knew the most likely spots where it could be found, which often meant covering many miles—not infrequently in vain—or risking life and limb in the topmost branches of a lofty elm. I recall, too, the names we had for some of the birds. A hedge sparrow was either a "hedge bet" or a "moper", a missel-thrush a "felfet", a house sparrow a "spitty", a starling a "starchy", a song-thrush a "mavis", and a whitethroat a "chat", while magpies were known as "maggies" and wagtails as "nanny washtails".

Looking back, I shudder to think of the things we used to take from the hedgerows and eat—and with relish. The buds of hawthorn were much sought after and known to us as bread and

The only buildings on the left-hand side of Station Road when this photograph was taken were Hill House and Egypt Cottage. The row of trees, mainly elms, stretched from the entrance to Mill Field all the way to Foundry Lane.

cheese, and the succulent young growth of wild rose bushes, another delicacy, we knew as roast beef. The berries of the hawthorn, correctly known as haws, we knew as "harsies", and those we found most tasty were the large dark red variety. These were held in much higher esteem than the smaller lighter-red berries and aspired to the name of "butter harsies", and we knew the bushes on which they grew. Rose hips, when ripe, were not so popular, because of the hairy nature of the seeds they contained. Other titbits to be taken when the opportunity presented itself were kohlrabi, locust beans—which were occasionally fed to cattle—and maize, or sweet corn, taken from where it grew in the fields.

Thinking back on those days brings to mind various field and place names heard today only from the lips of the older natives of the town. The Hungerdowns was about six acres of scrubland, long since cleared and cultivated, an excellent habitat for a wide variety of birds and a well-known spot for blackberrying. It was immediately north of the railway line about midway between Burnham and Althorne stations, and opposite what we knew as the Third Cliff, which was yet another haunt much favoured for picnics or a day's camping. The abundance of driftwood ensured there would be no shortage of fuel to keep camp fires going.

Hammocks Shed, which has long since fallen into decay and disappeared, was on the marshes between Newman's Farm and Goldsand Bridges, a Southminster marsh farm. This old open barn, with its mouldering thatch, frequently housed pigs, and it was not surprising that when we visited this outpost of our stamping ground to clamber along the dust-covered beams to search the thatch for sparrows' nests we became flea infested. We used to strip off in an adjoining field and give all our clothes a good shaking to rid them of lodgers.

Cats Wood was the name given to the stand of trees now within St Mary's School playground and an adjoining overgrown pond and patch of scrubland on the north side of Iron Bridge; an area of trees and bushes, mostly furze, which surrounded a pond in the Creeksea area was known colloquially as The Fuzz. Field names included Pig Marsh, The Pical, Long Poplars, Bricklamps and The Hoppet.

We went freshwater fishing, mainly for roach, in a number of ponds, including Sharps Pond in Greenlanes, Creeksea Lodge Pond and Kendalls Pond in Creeksea Road, and Creeksea Church pond, now within Burnham golf course. More risky fishing sorties were in the ponds in the fine grounds of Creeksea Place; as an added bonus for the risk taken one could obtain a useful fishing pole from the bamboo which grew there. Larger game in the shape of fine tench were the prize, but although the ponds were well stocked very few of these tantalizing fish were ever hooked.

Another pond was in Littlejohns Wood, a fine wood in the Ostend hinterland which the owner was, quite wrongly I feel, given permission to remove on the condition that he improved Lords Wood, another wood owned by him on the Old Heath Road. In the field adjoining Littlejohns Wood was what we knew as the Island Pond, so named because of the small island in its centre, and another pond we visited was the fine well-reeded pond at Goldsand

Chapel Road looking north from the Witney Road junction in the early nineteen-hundreds.

73

Bridges, which was an ideal haunt for many kinds of water-loving birds. Our usual route to this Southminster marshes pond was by the railway line from Iron Bridge, under Marsh Bridge, over Jackdaw Bridge (so named because this was a nesting site for jackdaws), and on until in sight of Southminster goods sheds and opposite a wood near Goldsands Farm. Here we forsook the railway line to skirt the wood and cross the road to our goal. Other sorties were by the seawall route to the low-lying fields beyond Althorne railway station, much used as a nesting site by plovers, and the Fambridge marshes, which were particularly rich in birdlife.

When older folk say that the weather pattern has changed over the years and claim that winters are not nearly so severe as they were half a century ago, their remarks are often received with scepticism by the younger generation. But in the days of my youth ice skating on the various local ponds and ditches was a regular and eagerly anticipated winter pastime. Those not fortunate enough to own a pair of skates contented themselves with either sliding on the ice or enjoying a good laugh when any of the less practised skaters came to grief. Skates made of wood apart from the steel blade, which were screwed on to the heel of the boot and strapped across the toes, could be purchased locally for around two shillings a pair. What excitement there was among youngsters when the word travelled like wildfire through the school that "The Pits pond bears"! There was a rush at the end of school hours to what in those days was a very sizeable pond in the gravel pits, so conveniently close to the Devonshire Road school. The pond with its surrounding well-bushed area was a popular playground for the "up-streeters". It was fed by a fast-running stream which ran under the railway line and linked Cats Wood pond with The Pits pond.

During the 1914–18 war the Army dug trenches in the high and then broad area of flat ground at the eastern side of The Pits, an area known to us youngsters as "The Mount", and when hostilities were over what an exciting new dimension these trenches provided us youngsters with for our games. As they had plenty of cover The Pits provided an excellent nesting site for birds and was regularly frequented by both nightingales and "butcher birds" or red-backed shrikes, which over the past decades seem to have completely deserted the area.

This unspoilt pocket of land was not improved when its northern boundary became the dumping ground for the town's household rubbish, although it did serve the purpose of making up the access road from Eastern Road to the field north of The Pits, where there was a sand pit. The Pits, alas, is yet another of Burnham's open spaces which the planners have sacrificed on the altar of progress, and it has now become Hester Place.

Sports and Pastimes 11

PROBABLY the first organized game played in Burnham was cricket, and the first club the Burnham Cricket Club, which folded when its ground on Saltcourts was taken by the Royal Corinthian Yacht Club for its dinghy park.

One of the cricket club's old minute books sheds interesting light on its activities around the time of the First World War. At the annual meeting held at the Star Hotel in 1913 under the chairmanship of Mr F. R. Wooster, who lived at The Barn in Church Road, which was demolished in 1973, Mr H. G. Makin agreed to be captain provided he received obedience on the field and that there was no talking during matches. Mr John Auger, who featured prominently in the club's batting honours for a great many years, was elected vice-captain. The club hired Saltcourts from Mr Percy Pipe, of Hill Farm, Burnham, and later of Mansion House Farm, Althorne, the tenant of Sir Henry Mildmay, and sub-let part of the field to Burnham Tennis Club at £4 a year. As the tennis club sub-let its part of the field to Burnham Rifle Club, it was proposed that the tennis club's annual rent be raised to £6 a year. This proposal was defeated and an amendment that the tennis club should no longer be allowed to sub-let and that the rifle club rent their part of the field directly from the cricket club was carried.

Mr Gordon Ambrose, who was elected assistant secretary, was another of the club's stalwarts both on the field of play—where his round arm deliveries played great havoc with the opposing batsmen—and on the administrative side. He was still secretary when the club came to the end of its illustrious career.

In 1915, when the balance sheet showed a balance of 5s 9d, it was decided to play a few matches during the war years to keep the club ticking over and to keep members together. Mr H. J. Cooke agreed to hire the field and seawall for grazing sheep at £5 a year. A complaint was made that Nethercoat's cows were causing damage by straying on to the playing pitch, and notice was served that unless this was stopped proceedings would be taken. Captain Jackson of Creeksea Place, who was president of the club, later became its landlord and in 1919 gave the club notice to quit.

In 1920 Mildmay Cricket Club was formed and sought amalgamation with the Burnham club, but this did not materialize and Mildmay obtained its own ground. In the same year it was agreed

Burnham tradesmen's cricket team in the late nineteenth century. Descendants of several of these old sportsmen still live in the town.

to have a hundred fixture cards printed at a cost of 18s. It seemed that at the annual meetings business was combined with pleasure, as a suggestion by the Reverend T. C. Smith that the meetings be held somewhere other than in a public house was turned down. About this time the club had a very strong team with two particularly devastating opening bowlers in G. (Spero) Stebbings and Fred (Brock) Harvey, who on one occasion dismissed the home team—Foulness Island—for two runs (one run plus one bye!). Their bowling figures were: Stebbings 6 for 1, Harvey 4 for 0.

A question often asked, but so far as I can ascertain seldom if ever satisfactorily answered, is when organized football was first played in Burnham. I am satisfied that I have come up with the right answer from the yellowing pages of the first local newspaper of the district—the monthly *Burnham-on-Crouch and Dengie Hundred Review*.

Football is mentioned in the very first issue, published in April, 1895.

To what an alarming extent football fever has spread to Burnham! All ages seem to have been affected by it, down to small schoolboys, who have been learning to charge, pass, dribble and shoot goals in Burnham High Street to the imminent danger of shop windows and pedestrians. The town club has certainly little cause to be ashamed of the form it has displayed in this, the first season of its existence. Until last October several members of the team had hardly seen, let alone kicked a football and were absolutely ignorant of the rules of the game, but they have made good use of their time since and 'Skipper' Staines is to be congratulated on the result. True the club has had to put up with one or two severe drubbings, but in no match has the team been disgraced. It is a credit to the club, too, that it knows how to accept defeat. This has been remarked upon by more than one of the teams which have been fortunate enough to lower its colours. Nothing looks worse in any sport than to wrangle over every point against you and to lose your temper with the game.

Reading through these truisms on sportsmanship written over ninety years ago, I could not help wondering what the writer's thoughts would be to see how some players of today behave on the field and how they react to referees' decisions.

The Town was not the only football club in Burnham. There was also a team known as Burnham Rovers, but little seems to have been recorded of their activities. The Rovers played their home matches on a field at Burnham Wick, loaned to them by Messrs A. and W. Croxon, while the Town team's ground was a field in Ship Road (probably Martin's Meadow) owned by William Newman.

Even in those early days spectator trouble was raising its ugly head, as the following comments in the *Burnham-on-Crouch and Dengie Hundred Review* on a Burnham Rovers versus Southend Swifts match go to show:

> Strangers to Burnham who watched the Burnham Rovers match on Good Friday must have been astounded at the eccentricities of its 'natives' and the outrageous behaviour of many of the boys who formed a considerable portion of the spectators. Whenever the ball went out of play 20 or 30 of these young hopefuls seized upon it and had a game on their own account, the rival teams having in the meantime to suspend operations. A remarkable thing is that four highly intelligent and sportsmanlike fathers encouraged their sons in these unheard of proceedings, and offered to alter the shape of the face of the Burnham club's secretary for interfering.

In its first season the Town club was a late starter; it was not

Burnham Town football team in 1899—probably the earliest photograph of a Burnham football team in existence. Back row, left to right: Ebenezer Dilliway (secretary), Jack Clarke, Ted Bourne, George Yardley, George Martin, Owen Westhorp, Tom Nethercoat, Charlie Cundy (linesman). Front row: Tom Yardley, Harry Yardley, Walter Hawkes, Jack Hawkes, Tommy Taylor.

The Wanderers, a team of twelve- to fourteen-year-olds who were winners of a football given by Burnham Ramblers Football Club in a three-match competition with the Swifts, another boys' team, in 1920. Back row, left to right: John Wright, Herbert Wilkinson, Leslie Harvey. Middle row: Tib Mitchell, Jack Clark, Richard Mellard, Brian Carter, Stanley King. Front row: Arthur Cole, George Clarke, Leslie Crix, Ernie Perry, Ronald Brown.

formed until the season had well begun, and most of the players still had to learn the game. But they were quick off the mark for the 1895–96 season, when they had a greater number of fixtures.

It appears that even in those early days the shortage of football grounds presented a problem. At the close of the 1895–96 season the ground at Burnham Wick was closed. Commenting on the need for playing space, the *Review* remarks:

> Burnham now has a football club without a ground, but the town also possesses a wide High Street and the traffic is not very heavy. Naturally, therefore, in the absence of a field, it has been selected as the most suitable spot for football.

The end of this season was certainly an eventful occasion for the Town club, as not only did it lose its ground but also its captain, "Skipper" Staines, who resigned claiming that he was sworn at by some of the members at the match against Southend Rovers on Christmas Day, when he acted as referee. He also objected to the roughness of the play on that occasion. The following season the Burnham Rovers and Town clubs amalgamated under the name of Burnham United, with George Yardley as captain and J. Staines

and F. Harvey as joint secretaries. Because members of ordinary benefit clubs were not entitled to any payments in respect of accidents while playing football, a football slate club was formed from which members disabled while playing football in a match were entitled to an allowance of five shillings a week!

It was not long before three teams were again playing on the field at Burnham Wick—Burnham United, Burnham Swifts and Burnham Ramblers, the latter a team of younger players formed in 1900. The Swifts do not seem to have survived very long. Later Burnham United moved to Mill Field (the field now occupied by Warwick Court flatlets and Burnham Sports clubhouse) and Burnham Ramblers to Brickwall Field (now Brickwall Close). When United disbanded the Ramblers moved to Mill Field where they stayed until 1925, when thanks to the generosity of their president (the late Mr Robert Leslie) they purchased their ground in Silver Road.

I played for the Ramblers on both fields, and this move was a great step forward from the players' point of view. Mill Field was notoriously bad, with furrows usually full of water, the goalmouths ankle deep in mud and the rest of the field well plastered with cow pats. (The field was also used as a grazing ground for the dairy herd of Jack Nethercoat, who had a dairy in Silver Road.) Spectators were able to keep reasonably clean by using the duckboards provided by the club. All round the field were ditches usually well filled with water, and when the ball landed in these—which was quite often—it had to be retrieved by means of an iron hoop on the end of a long pole. Clubs did not run to a second match ball in those days, which meant that the match was held up while the ball recovery exercise was in progress. Repeated duckings made the leather balls heavy and slippery and very difficult to control. There was no dressing room on the ground, and players turned up with a coat over their togs; the coats were folded and left in the back of one of the goal nets during the match.

With United disbanded and the Swifts fallen by the wayside the Ramblers were Burnham's only team until 1908, when Mildmay Ironworks' team was formed, and immediately there started a great rivalry which often had feelings running high between the teams' followers. This continued, although later to a lesser degree, until the Mildmay club disbanded. When first formed Mildmay's home ground was Hill Field, immediately north of Mill Field, stretching from the public library to the top of the hill and bounded on the north by the public footpath leading to Creeksea.

The competitions entered by the two Burnham teams were the Essex Junior Cup and the Wickford and District League. The latter later became the South-East Essex League, and when this was eventually disbanded through lack of support the handsome trophy was presented to the Dengie Hundred Minor League, which was formed in the late nineteen-fifties. After the South-East Essex League the two Burnham teams competed in the North Essex League, of which the Ramblers were champions in 1927–28, 1928–29 and 1930–31 and runners-up in the 1926–27 and 1932–33 seasons. For several seasons both teams also entered the Chelmsford and District League, of which the Ramblers were champions in 1927–28.

This remarkable run of success made the Ramblers rather ambitious and they looked for fresh fields and pastures new. They decided on the much stronger South Essex League, but here they met with moderate success and withdrew after only a few seasons. The highly competitive Southend and District League was also given a trial, but this was very much the domain of Southminster St Leonards. Local teams certainly took more than their share of the spoils in this purple patch from the mid nineteen-twenties to the early nineteen-thirties.

The Ramblers club sold its Silver Road ground for housing and opened the 1987–88 season at its new ground in Springfield Road.

A red letter day in Burnham's sporting calendar in the early

Burnham Ramblers line up against their opponents on their old ground in Wick Road. The club has since moved to a ground in Springfield Road, and a residential estate covers the site of the old pitch.

nineteen-hundreds was the terrier coursing held on Boxing Day at Burnham Wick on a field lent by Mr Arthur Croxon. One of the local publicans would erect a marquee and set up barrels of beer, and the longer the meeting continued the drunker everyone became and the higher went the bets between owners. There were never so many drunk dredgermen as on these occasions.

This was very much a working man's sport, and because they could not run to the expense of beaters to drive up hares they settled for the next best thing—rabbits previously netted in the vicinity. When a rabbit was liberated the dogs were slipped in pairs and the final winner was arrived at by a knock-out process. Some of the dogs entered were the longest-legged terriers one could imagine and would probably have stood a greater chance of success if entered in the greyhound class at Crufts than they would have done in the terrier section. Among the regular competing owners were Sam Bridge, F. Rogers, George Chipperfield, William Hawes, Fisher Warren, Joe Death, Alf Hawkes, C. C. Booth, Sid Barker, W. Burrows and Owen Westhorp.

Most of the games we played as youngsters seemed to have their seasons. A regular was kite flying (the kites were home constructed affairs made from a lath, a piece of cane, brown paper, string and flour-and-water paste) in which the ambition of every kite flyer was to become "King of the field". This meant getting your kite to fly higher than any other, which with anything up to twenty in the same field often meant entanglements. The first owner of the two kites involved to cry "my first cut" would have the privilege of cutting the other's string to free his own kite. A common cause of a kite suddenly losing height was a slipping "bellyband", an expression which will certainly mean little to the uninitiated. The "bellyband" was the cord to which the string was made fast.

There were two types of hoops—wooden ones knocked along by a stick for the girls and iron ones with a slider for the boys. A slight variation in vogue at the same time as hoops was a small perambulator wheel with an iron bolt or a piece of wood projecting about a couple of inches from one side of the hub, which was propelled and controlled by a stick placed under the projection. Other regular games were marbles, tops (either shop-bought "jam jars" or wasp-waisted "flying Dutchies" fashioned from cotton reels) and conkers, which we used to bake to make really hard.

Perhaps most popular of all with the boys were billymot and woggle, games which have long since died out and are not even known by the younger generation. Woggle was a team game for any number of players and was not without its dangers. Very broadly speaking it had some resemblance to cricket, with sticks for bats and two holes some five inches in diameter and about nine feet apart for the pitch. Instead of a ball a "woggle", a five-inch-long piece of wood an inch or a little more in diameter, was used. The two bowlers of the fielding side would attempt to get the "woggle" into the opposite end hole. If the striker succeeded in sending the "woggle" on its way—not always an easy task when close-herded by a "field" set suicidally close in—the two strikers would make as many runs as they could by crossing between the two holes before the "woggle" was returned to the bowler.

If a batsman was proving difficult to dislodge the bowlers would be advised by their team mates to vary the bowling by giving him an "orchard drop", a high delivery which they hoped would drop in the hole, or a "grass cutter", a very low delivery, which as its name implies never left the ground. If a bowler succeeded in getting the "woggle" to land in the hole the two bowlers would go a distance away with their backs to the batsmen; returning with their hands stuffed up their jersey fronts, one of them with the "woggle", they would crouch low over the holes. The one without the "woggle" would, of course, stick his thumb out to give the impression that he and not his companion had it under his jersey. The strikers then had to take a chance on who held the "woggle" and attempt to change ends before it could be slipped into a hole. If they failed, one of the batsmen was out. Various methods were used by the batsmen to help them make the important decision of which bowler held the "woggle". Some would tug hairs from their forelock with both hands and then make their choice according to which hand held the most hairs. Others would spit on the back of the one hand and then smartly tap the spit with the forefinger of the other. The spit would fly in two directions and where the greater volume landed decided for him where the "woggle" should be.

By comparison billymot was a far less hazardous game, although even it had its dangers if a player stood too close to his opponent when an attempt at a big hit was being made. The pitch for this was a circle about two feet in diameter drawn in the earth, in the centre of which stood the "mot", a thin piece of stick some three inches long. Standing about eight feet from the circle, the bowler would lob the "billy," a four-inch-long piece of wood an inch thick and pointed at both ends, in an attempt to knock down the "mot". If he succeeded his opponent was out and it was his turn to bowl, but if the "billy" landed outside the circle his opponent was allowed three hits; on the line meant two hits and in the circle one. A hit consisted of the striker tapping the pointed end of the "billy" with his stick and attempting to strike it away from the circle as it rose in the air. The score made was the number of jumps allowed by the striker for the bowler to jump from wherever the "billy" had landed to the circle. If the bowler managed to jump into the circle in fewer jumps than the number he had been allowed, the striker was out.

"Kicky-man-policeman" and "relievo" were other games which

Floods have always proved a hazard in Burnham. Water lapped at the doors of the White Harte in 1965 when a high tide flooded parts of the Quay.

were always popular, but during the summer months much time was spent in swimming or in mucking about on the waterfront. Two guessing games, played on winter evenings by the light of the street gas lamps, were "Fool, fool, come home from school" and "guessies". For the latter the initial letters of sweets on display in a shop window were used. In the former game the player who was to become the "fool" was decided upon in various ways, one of the most popular being for the players to stand in a circle each with a finger held lightly round the inside of a boy's cap. At the sudden command "let go" the players had to hold on and when the command was "hold tight" they had to let go and the player who was first to make a mistake became the "fool". The other players, sitting on a fence, were each given the name of a bird and the "fool" was told: "Fool, fool, come home from school and pick me out the . . ." A bird's name was given. When the "fool" made the wrong choice he was chased back to "school" and called again and again to select some other bird until he made the right choice, when the player chosen became the "fool."

Simple games, but they kept us out of mischief.

Folk Fought for their Rights

12

IN YEARS gone by Burnham folk were jealous of their heritage and would not let anything be taken from them without a fight. In 1902, when a Mr Smith erected a fence to prevent public access to part of the Quay in an attempt to establish that frontagers owned the Quay and were responsible for its upkeep, ratepayers led by Mr Ebenezer Dilliway, founder and first editor of the *Burnham and Dengie Advertiser* and for many years clerk to the council, demolished the fence. Mr Dilliway was threatened with legal action as a result. Several stormy public meetings culminated in the council's seeking legal advice, with the result that it was established that as the Quay had been open to the public for so many years it had become a public right of way and it was the duty of the council to keep it in repair and to prevent any encroachment. The threatened legal action against Mr Dilliway was not proceeded with.

In this instance public outcry and the action of one man prevented part of the Quay being lost to the public, but the outcome was not so satisfactory in the case of the disputed public right of way along the foot of the seawall over what was later the forecourt of the Royal Corinthian Yacht Club's dormitory block. The matter was spotlighted in 1898, when the Burnham Yacht Building Company proposed to hire from the Burnham Charity Trustees the wharf and quay where the coastguard vessel *Kangaroo* was formerly stationed (now the site of the Royal Corinthian clubhouse). The company applied to the council for permission to restrict the right of way which the council had over the land to a width of ten feet. The upper floor of the building, to have been used as a yacht clubhouse, would have extended across the right of way, leaving a covered walkway for members of the public.

The members of the council could not agree that a public right of way did exist over the land and the matter was adjourned. The outcome was that the proposed buildings were never erected and the public lost what seemed at that time to have been a public right of way. Several years later the trustees of Burnham Charity sold a forty foot plot of ground with frontage to Belvedere Road and including the right of way to the Royal Corinthian Yacht Club for

Opposite page:
Burnham residents taking the law into their own hands in 1902 and removing a fence with which part of the Quay had been enclosed. A policeman looks on, apparently content to let matters take their course.

Creeksea Ferry, with the raised walkway which led down to low water mark.

£120. Much of this plot later formed the open space in front of the club's dormitory block.

Many years later Burnham folk again lost out when after a public inquiry a favourite picnic spot at Creeksea, to which they had enjoyed undisputed access since time immemorial, was purchased for private development and the footpath diverted off the seawall to make the only break in the seawall footpath between Bradwell and Fambridge. More recently the use of part of the saltings and foreshore at Creeksea, to which again the public had enjoyed undisputed access since time immemorial, has been denied the public. This was disappointingly surrendered without the council or public making a fight of it.

Political meetings seemed to engender far more heat among supporters of the various parties in earlier days, particularly in the run up to a General Election. At one meeting held in the Public Hall in High Street (now the Electricity Board's showroom) in support of the Labour Party an ardent Labour supporter openly accused an equally ardent supporter of the Tory cause of dropping stink bombs, an accusation which ended in a punch-up. On another occasion a keen supporter of one of the candidates was in trouble for painting unacceptable slogans on the highway—slogans which he suffered the humiliation of being forced to remove. As youngsters we would put words either praising or discrediting election candidates—according to the particular political persuasion of our parents—to some well-known tune and sing them round the streets.

Above: *A wintry view of boats moored at the Quay. The boarded shed on the left is the one which can just be seen on the right of the photograph on page 84.*

Right: *The North Sea floods of 31st January and 1st February, 1953, carried away the wooden upper portion of the sea wall. This photograph taken on 1st February shows how the rush of water had lifted huge slabs of road surfacing and carried them along. On the extreme right can be seen the steps of the war memorial.*

Taking Stock 13

A WORLD-WIDE upsurge in population and never-ending advances in technology have played a major role in changing our way of life during the course of the present century; nowhere is this more true than in rural areas. Only when the present-day way of life is compared to that of half a century or more ago can we begin to realize just how far we have travelled along a road that some of us would, perhaps, prefer not to have taken.

As the country lurches from crisis to crisis, as one union or another causes disruption by ordering its members to strike—or sometimes provokes a crisis by merely threatening to do so—I am led to question whether the quality of life of our forebears was much worse than ours today, despite the tremendous technological advances that have been made.

In the early years of this century Burnham was described as a parish consisting of 5,523 acres, bounded by the German Ocean (the First World War which changed so much was responsible for a change of name to the North Sea) and the River Crouch on the east and south and by the parishes of Southminster and Althorne on the north and west. That is still basically true today, but so much else has changed.

The population was then a little under three thousand. By 1971 the number of people living in the parish had grown to 4,619, and today there are about 7,000 inhabitants, many of whom find employment not in Burnham but many miles away. Yet the story of the century has not been in every way one of upward progress.

If the number of places of worship is any criterion there has been a distinct falling off in the town of the emphasis placed on religion. There used to be eight places of worship in the town: St Mary's Church, the Congregational church, which until it was destroyed by fire in 1946 stood at the corner of High Street and Chapel Road, the Baptist Chapel on the corner of Station Road and York Road, the Primitive Methodist Chapel in Albert Road, the Strict Baptist Chapel in Belvedere Road, the Catholic Apostolic Church in Providence, the Marsh Mission, started in 1895 thanks to the efforts of Burnham builder Mr J. W. Jones, and the Salvation Army, whose original headquarters was at the rear of Warners Hall in High Street. Today only three of these remain, although the town does now also have a Roman Catholic Church.

Opposite page: Tidal flooding in November, 1897, left High Street looking like a Venetian canal. Because of its situation beside the River Crouch the lower part of the town has always suffered from periodic flooding.

It is not only in the matter of Sunday observance that habits have changed. Once only "best clothes" were worn on Sundays; now it is very much a matter of "anything goes". Indeed, of the many changes seen over the years, not the least is in the matter of dress. Gone are the leather buskins once popular with both men and boys, and gone too are the spats worn by the bowler-hat brigade who commuted to London by train. The jerseys worn by the majority of schoolboys when I was a youngster have been superseded by sweat shirts and anoraks. Women's knee-length button-up boots, which had to be laboriously fastened up with a button hook, have given way to the much more convenient and speedy zip-up knee boots. Today's women must feel far freer in the foundation garments of today than did their forebears in their restricting boned lace-up corsets, and how much more convenient must be briefs than the lace-trimmed white cotton drawers with button-up back flap worn by the schoolgirls of my generation.

A busy scene in one of the machine shops at Mr Tom Nethercoat's sailmaking works during the First World War.

Although we did not realize what was happening at the time, the 1914–18 war was responsible for a considerable change in women's life and expectations. Many local girls and housewives were employed during the war at the local sailmakers' establishments turning out canvas tents, buckets and other items needed for the Forces, and those housewives unable to put in a full day in such places took work home and did it in their spare time. A corrugated iron building, later moved to Queens Road to become the Queens Hall, was erected in New Road next to Alpha House to serve as an emergency hospital. It was staffed by volunteer Red Cross nurses who did good work in caring for wounded servicemen.

Generally the war had little impact on us youngsters, although there was some excitement one day in 1917 when twenty-two German Gotha bombers droned in from the east on their way to London. They passed directly over the town and we watched as shells from the anti-aircraft guns stationed at the Wick burst

Canvas buckets made in Mr Tom Nethercoat's works during the First World War are inspected before being delivered to the Forces.

The Coastguard station with launching ramp for the Coastguards' boats in front. The Royal Corinthian Yacht Club now occupies the site.

around the raiders. We also turned out, if the raid was before bedtime, when zeppelins made a night raid, watching excitedly as searchlights lanced the night skies searching for these silver-coloured monsters.

The passing years have certainly brought no improvement in the town's postal services, which used to include three deliveries and four despatches of mail daily in winter. The telegraph office was open from eight in the morning to eight at night each weekday and from eight to ten on Sunday mornings.

One also notes that before the turn of the century the strength of the local police was considerably greater than it is today, despite the population having more than doubled. In those far-off days the town could boast an inspector, a sergeant and a constable; at the turn of the century the local policemen were Inspector A. Rome, Sergeant W. Cowell and Pc A. Rolfe. I find it difficult to believe that the establishment has been reduced because we have all become so much more law-abiding.

This century has seen the withdrawal of resident coastguard personnel, who before the erection of the coastguard cottages in Silver Road had been housed with their families on the watch vessel *Kangaroo*, which was moored to the sea wall on the site on which the Royal Corinthian Yacht Club now stands.

At least the district is by no means as isolated as it was during much of the nineteenth century, for up to 1895 the only link with the outside world was the town carrier, Mr J. Nethercoat, who piloted his horse-drawn carrier's van to Chelmsford every Friday, starting out at seven in the morning and returning the same day.

Right: *The Coastguard watch vessel* Kangaroo, *which came to Burnham in 1874 to replace the* **Chanticleer** *and was moored where the Royal Corinthian Yacht Club now stands. She was removed in 1896.*

Below: *The old Royal Corinthian Yacht Club on the Quay, burnt down in 1914.*

The Wickford–Southminster railway was opened in 1895, the first ticket to be issued at Burnham Station being purchased by Mr John Smith, who was then chairman of the parish council. The branch line continues to serve Burnham and the surrounding area in an age when so many of the town's residents have cars and so much freight is carried by road.

In the field of education there have certainly been great strides forward. In 1895 the only public place of education was the charity or National School, the accommodation of which was quite inadequate for the number of children attending; even in those far-off days the Education Department was pressing the parish to provide more places. Private education for those who could afford it was available at an infants' school conducted by a Mrs T. Smith at Hillside and at the Collegiate School at what is now Warners Hall in High Street.

Burnham station in the early nineteen-seventies, after the waiting room and other buildings on the up platform had been removed. The remains of the footbridge linking the two platforms can still be seen.

Seventy years and more ago the curriculum at Burnham's council school (where teachers, immaculately turned out themselves, were not slow to tell youngsters to smarten themselves up if it was necessary) did not extend much beyond the "Three Rs", history, geography and nature study. Sex education, of which I feel too much is heard today, was certainly not included. In the

country, close to nature, it was perhaps felt to be unnecessary; I am convinced few left school without knowing rather more than they should have done about the facts of life. Sex was a subject never discussed in the home, and the scanty advice occasionally given by parents to their offspring was on the earthy side, to say the least.

Something which has always stuck in my mind is the admonishment given by my mother to one of my school-aged sisters when she started to show an interest in the opposite sex: "You silly little fool, you want to go and stick your backside in a pail of cold water." Yes, she was a strict disciplinarian who did not have a cane as an ornament, and we had it firmly driven home what was right and what was wrong; perhaps we are none the worse off for it.

At school in those days far less emphasis was placed on sport than it is today; organized games were not introduced until the early nineteen-twenties, when they were restricted to an hour on Wednesday afternoons. The older boys played football on a field loaned by local farmer Mr Wilfred Newman, on the Marsh Road side of the Iron Bridge; before a game could be started goalposts had to be manhandled from the school and erected, and taken back when the game ended. The older girls played netball on the asphalted part of the playground.

There is no doubt that today's rising generation is being given a very different education from that which was meted out to us, in very different buildings from those in which we were taught. I

Left: *Motor torpedo boats and other craft were built for the Royal Navy during the Second World War in these sheds belonging to William King and Sons.*

Below: *A supermarket now stands on the site once occupied by this old cottage and shop in Station Road.*

hope that perhaps this book will be read by today's younger generation so that they will understand how much more spartan and yet how much more carefree was the life of their forebears.

Because of its potential as a yachting centre Burnham must expect, and must accept, a degree of change, but in fairness to the residential population of the town as a whole changes must not be allowed to rob the "locals" of their traditional rights or deprive them of their heritage.

Burnham folk, particularly the older people among them, were sad when in the late nineteen-sixties The Lawns on the corner of High Street and Belvedere Road was demolished. The subsequent development of the site brought them little cheer, the consensus of opinion being that the "new look" robbed the locality of much of its old charm. Before the bulldozers moved in, Belvedere Road had been a little-used thoroughfare without footpaths, bounded on the west side for its entire length by a high brick wall which in places was covered with ivy and overhung by evergreens, fig trees and towering elms.

In its earlier days the road could indeed boast a belvedere, from which the coastguards were able to keep an eye on river traffic and

Burnham Carnival Hall in Arcadia Road, built by public subscription. It is today performing the task done in the past by the Coronation Hall and the Queen's Hall.

97

from which owners of oyster layings could have watch kept on their layings, which sometimes attracted the attention of poachers from further up the coast, particularly from Brightlingsea.

The road was then used largely by farm waggons off-loading hay on to barges berthed immediately west of where the Royal Corinthian Yacht Club now stands. That trade, once so important to the capital city as well as to this corner of Essex, is now merely a memory, and Belvedere Road is today a very different kind of thoroughfare. Its past beauties should not be forgotten.

These sheds in Coronation Road formed part of the boatbuilding yard of Tucker Brown and Company; they have now been demolished. The left-hand shed was built by Mr John Hawkes and for many years served the town as the Coronation Hall.

A knowledge of the way of life in Burnham from the turn of the century onwards, and now changed for ever, lives only in the memories of the older generation. It is that thought which has prompted me to write this book, which I hope will recall long-forgotten memories to my contemporaries and give insight into the past to the younger generation.

I have a great pride, shared by many, in my home town, a pride which in times of need engenders a great spirit of co-operation and loyalty, embracing all sections of the community, as was so aptly proved in two world wars. Long may this spirit continue.

Above: *The clubhouse of the Burnham Yacht Club as it used to be.*

Right: *The crew of the yacht* Woodbine, *all Burnham men. Left to right they are: George Taylor, master; George Tunbridge, steward; Arthur Shekyls, cabin boy; Albert Grimwade, mate. The* Woodbine *was a yawl of 37 tons Thames Measurement owned for many years by Mr R. J. Alabaster, who was a member of the Burnham, Royal Corinthian and Royal Southern yacht clubs.*

Index

Illustrations in **bold** *type*

INDEX